ICE

Chilling stories from a disappearing world

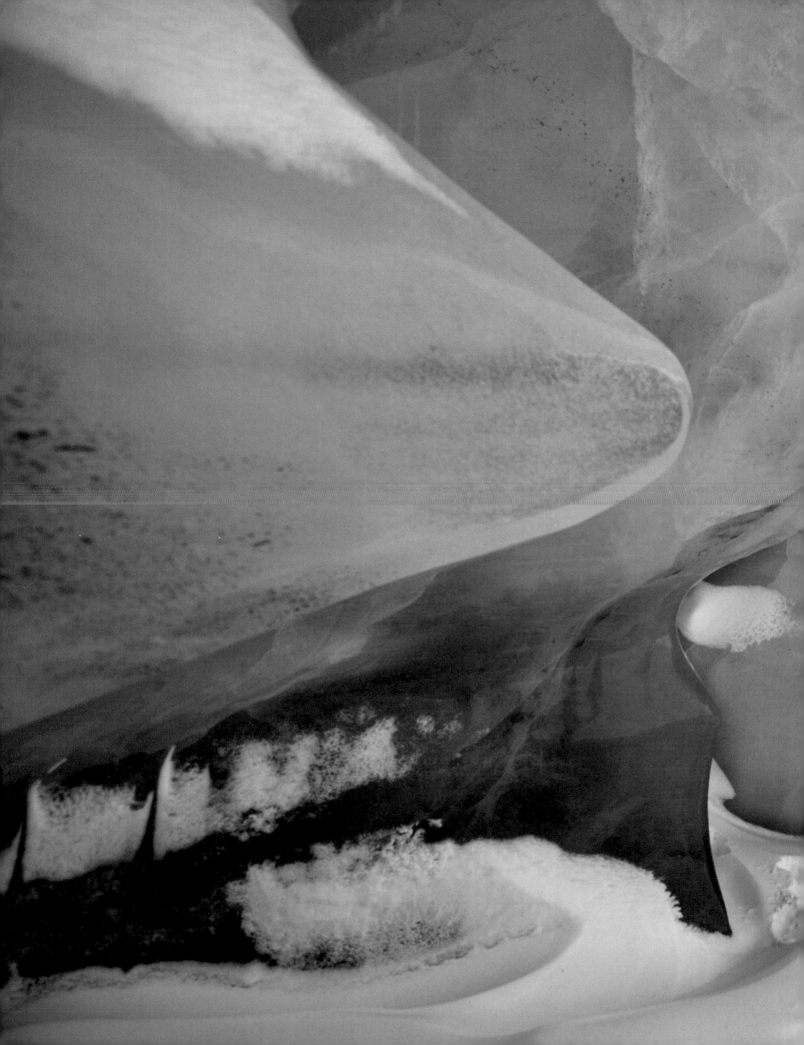

ICE

Chilling stories from a
disappearing world

Penguin
Random
House

Senior Editor Mani Ramaswamy
Senior Art Editor Jacqui Swan
Senior Editor Ben Morgan
Designers Sunita Gahir, Peter Radcliffe
US Editors Megan Douglass, Kayla Dugger, Lori Hand
Illustrators Gus Scott, Clarisse Hassan
DK Media Archive Romaine Werblow
Picture Researcher Laura Barwick
Managing Editor Lisa Gillespie
Managing Art Editor Owen Peyton Jones
Producer, Pre-Production Gillian Reid
Senior Producer Meskerem Berhane
Jacket Designers Surabhi Wadhwa-Gandhi, Suhita Dharamjit
Jackets Design Development Manager Sophia MTT
Jackets DTP Designer Rakesh Kumar
Jackets Editorial Coordinator Priyanka Sharma
Jackets Editor Emma Dawson
Managing Jackets Editor Saloni Singh
Publisher Andrew Macintyre
Art Director Karen Self
Associate Publishing Director Liz Wheeler
Design Director Phil Ormerod
Publishing Director Jonathan Metcalf

Written by Laura Buller, Andrea Mills, John Woodward
Consultants Peter Clarkson, Robert Dinwiddie, Derek Harvey

First American Edition, 2019
Published in the United States by DK Publishing
1450 Broadway, Suite 801, New York, NY 10018
Copyright © 2019 Dorling Kindersley Limited
DK, a Division of Penguin Random House LLC
19 20 21 22 23 10 9 8 7 6 5 4 3 2 1
001–312737–Sept/2019

A catalog record for this book
is available from the Library of Congress.
ISBN 978-1-4654-8170-2

Printed and bound in China

A WORLD OF IDEAS:
SEE ALL THERE IS TO KNOW

www.dk.com

MIX
Paper from
responsible sources
FSC™ C018179

C O N

PREHISTORY

TENTS

FROZEN WORLD

ANIMALS ON ICE

HUMANS ON ICE

ANIMAL FACTS

Each animal profile features all of the information shown in this box.

REGION/HABITAT
The region/habitat of the animal.

LENGTH/HEIGHT
The length/height of the animal, not including the tail.

WEIGHT
The weight of the animal.

CONSERVATION
The IUCN (International Union for Conservation of Nature) Red List status, which indicates the animal's global threat level.

INTRODUCTION

The icy regions of our planet are among its few truly wild places. They were the last parts of the world to be explored, thanks to their extreme climates and hostility to life. Indeed the great ice sheets of Greenland and Antarctica are the most lifeless places on Earth, but when winter loses its grip on the land, the melting snow reveals a landscape ready to burst into life.

In the Arctic, the thawing tundra starts to glow with color as plants race to flower and produce their seeds. Caribou and musk oxen enjoy a feast, and so do the packs of Arctic wolves that watch their every move. Vast flocks of birds that have flown north from warmer regions gather to lay their eggs and rear their chicks.

Just offshore, the seas teem with life, even beneath the floating pack ice. Clouds of plankton support great shoals of fish, which attract fish-eating seals, whales, and seabirds. Antarctic seas swarm with shrimplike animals called krill that are scooped up by huge whales, seals, and penguins, while powerful killer whales patrol the open

water looking for prey. In the Arctic, magnificent polar bears prowl the pack ice searching for seals to kill and devour, often shadowed by Arctic foxes hoping to feast on whatever the bears leave behind.

Mountains throughout the world have similar icy climates that make life hard or even impossible for plants and animals. The highest peaks are barren rock, snow, and ice, but their lower slopes are grassy meadows grazed by tough, sure-footed animals such as mountain goats. They are stalked by hunters like the snow leopard, while smaller animals are targeted by soaring birds of prey.

People have lived in some of these places for centuries, hunting, fishing, and herding. The world is changing, however. In particular, the way people live all over the globe is changing the climate. Polar seas that were once frozen throughout the year are now open water in summer, and icy landscapes and glaciers are melting away. Animals such as polar bears, which depend on the ice, may fade away, too, as their fragile world disappears beneath their feet. So we hope that this book will inspire you to help save these frozen worlds for future generations to marvel at, just as we do.

EXPLORING THE ICE
Wildlife camera crews venture into the wild to explore and reveal its secrets to us. Here, cameraman Gordon Buchanan films a pair of walruses from his kayak.

ICICLES

Icicles form when dripping water freezes into long spikes. They often form in shady places like the eaves of houses, where meltwater from the sunny roof cools back to freezing temperature.

Icicles can be deadly when they fall.

▲ Icebergs are giant blocks of floating ice in the sea.

▲ Glaciers are slow-moving "rivers" of ice that flow down mountains.

WHAT IS ICE?

Liquid water freezes into solid ice when the temperature drops to 32°F (0°C). Ice covers about 10 percent of Earth's land, mainly on mountains and at the poles. Ice on the polar oceans acts like a blanket, helping to maintain the temperature of the water below.

SOLID ICE

Ice floats because it is lighter (less dense) than liquid water. When water freezes, the molecules lock together in a hexagonal pattern. This takes up more space than liquid water, making it less dense.

HAILSTONES

Small, hard pellets of ice created inside thunderclouds fall to Earth as hailstones. These form when powerful air currents carry lumps of ice up and down inside the clouds. They grow in size until they become so heavy that they fall. Powerful storms can produce hailstones the size of tennis balls.

▲ The water under floating ice is warmer than the ice itself, allowing aquatic animals to survive in winter.

▲ As ice melts in the sunshine, different formations take shape naturally.

▲ Ice absorbs heat while melting, so ice cubes in a drink take in heat from the warmer liquid and cool it down.

PREHISTORY

Throughout its history, Earth has endured long phases when ice covered large areas of the planet. But life adapted to survive during those ice ages, the most recent of which ended only 10,000 years ago.

SNOWBALL EARTH

Many scientists agree that the coldest period in Earth's history happened between around 720 and 635 million years ago. Clues in rocks suggest that there were two severe ice ages, called "Snowball Earth" periods, when the entire planet froze over from pole to pole. Life on the surface of the land was wiped out, but microorganisms survived under the sea ice. Soon afterward, the first complex organisms began to appear.

THE ICE AGES

There have been at least five periods in Earth's history when the global climate has chilled and large areas have become covered by vast sheets of ice. These ice ages have lasted for millions of years, but each one has had colder and warmer phases. We are currently living in an ice age during which the ice sheets reached their greatest extent 23,000 years ago, but which has now entered a warmer phase.

THE LAST ICE AGE

At the peak of the most recent ice age, 23,000 years ago, the polar ice cap covered nearly all of Canada and northern Europe. Sea levels were lower than now, making coastlines different from today.

Scandinavia and most of the British Isles were buried under ice in the last ice age.

TODAY

We now live in a warmer period called an interglacial, which started around 10,000 years ago. Although the polar ice cap has retreated, there are still vast ice sheets covering Greenland and Antarctica.

LIVING IN THE ICE AGE

During the ice age, Arctic ice sheets spread south over northern Eurasia and America. To the south of the ice lay vast areas of ice-free grasslands grazed by bison, deer, wild horses, and mammoths. These were hunted by people, who used the hides to make clothes, and the bones and ivory to make tools and huts.

BONE SHELTER

Summers on the open grasslands were probably warm and dry, but winters could be bitterly cold. The people survived by building shelters, but since few trees grew on the plains, they used mammoth bones and tusks instead of wood.

Long, curved mammoth tusks supported the roof and formed a doorway.

Mammoth jawbones formed a strong framework that was covered with animal pelts to keep out the wind and rain.

MAMMOTH HUNTERS

In 1965, a farmer working at Mezhirich, near Kiev in Ukraine, discovered the remains of four shelters built by ice-age hunters. The buildings were made of the bones and tusks of at least 149 mammoths. Some of these may have been the remains of animals that had died of natural causes, but others were probably from mammoths that the hunters had killed.

The hunters used the bones to make tools as well as huts. Hunting weapons were made by striking one rock against another to knock off flakes that had sharp, knifelike edges.

These mammoth-bone huts are 14,500 years old, making them some of the earliest known dwellings made by people.

Around 3,000 years after the mammoth huts were built, the climate changed and the ice age came to an end.

END OF AN ERA

This bone hut is a reconstruction of the original, which collapsed thousands of years ago.

PREHISTORIC PAINTINGS

A chance discovery of a French cave in 1994 revealed one of the world's oldest collections of prehistoric art. Early people painted hundreds of images on the walls of the Chauvet Cave in the Ardèche region more than 30,000 years ago. Many of their paintings feature the animals they lived alongside during the last ice age, including cave bears, woolly mammoths, and Irish elks.

The walls were scraped to create a smooth surface before natural pigments made from dirt, spit, and animal fat were used to paint and bring the cave to life. Measuring 1,300 ft (400 m) in length, this vast cavern lay undisturbed for centuries, perfectly preserving its incredible images. Human footprints and the fossilized bones of animals that are now extinct were also found at the historic site.

▲ In some scenes, the animals appear to be charging or even fighting.

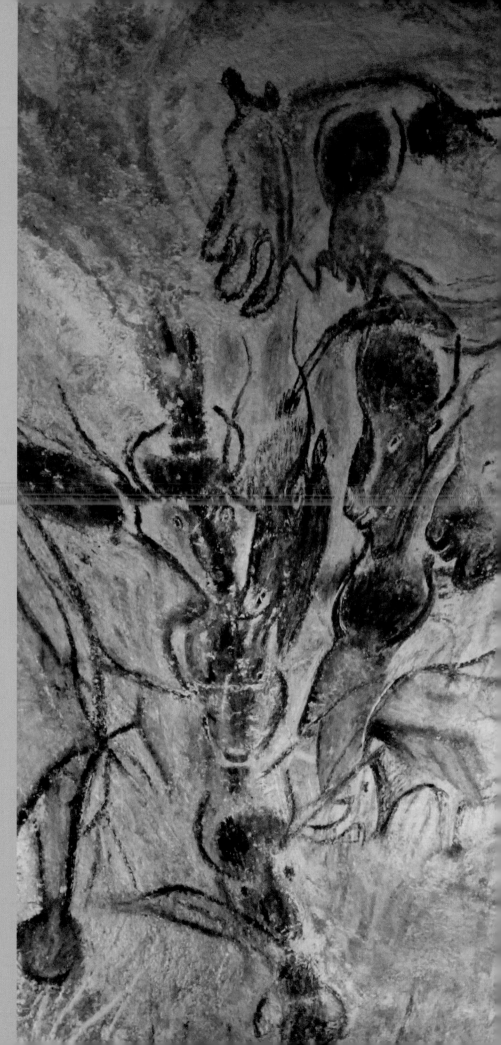

To minimize heat loss, mammoths had much smaller ears than modern elephants.

An outer layer of long, coarse hairs covered a shorter undercoat.

The tusks were elongated incisor teeth that grew up to 15 ft (4.5 m) long.

The soles of the feet were cracked to improve grip on slippery ice.

FROZEN IN TIME

Freezing cold temperatures and lasting ice in Siberia have helped preserve the past. Mummified bodies of woolly mammoths have been found in giant blocks of ice in almost perfect condition. Known as Lyuba, this baby died 42,000 years ago and was discovered in Siberia in 2007. She still had her mother's milk in her stomach.

Experts can figure out the age of a woolly mammoth by counting rings in the tusks.

MIGHTY MAMMOTH

Among the most magnificent animals of the last ice age were woolly mammoths. Although most died out 10,000 years ago, a tiny number survived until 4,000 years ago. Mammoth remains have been found across Europe, Asia, and North America. These massive mammals were ancient relatives of the modern elephant, similar in size and shape but better adapted to live in the cold.

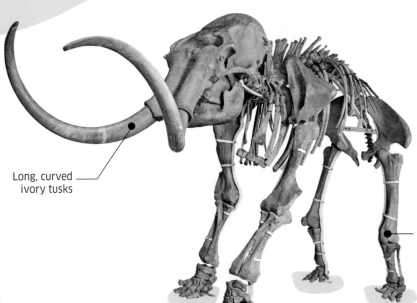

Long, curved ivory tusks

Stocky leg bones supported the enormous body weight.

SKELETON OF A WOOLLY MAMMOTH

Bones and tusks were used by prehistoric hunters to make tools and shelters.

MIGHTY TUSKS

The woolly mammoth was well adapted to the low temperatures of the ice age. Thick, shaggy hair and a deep layer of body fat trapped heat to provide warmth. The huge tusks were probably used for self-defense, attracting mates, and digging for food.

REGION/HABITAT
Asia/Europe

LENGTH
Up to 13 ft (4 m)

WEIGHT
2.2 tons

Shaggy outer
hairs covered a
dense undercoat.

GRAZING GIANTS

The woolly rhinoceros first appeared on Earth more than
3 million years ago and spread gradually across a wide area. This
species was a huge and hairy relative of modern rhinos. Ancient
cave paintings and frozen, fossilized remains help us learn about
this two-horned prehistoric beast. The chunky body and thick fur
were an essential survival kit during the ice age.

HAIRY HERBIVORE
Although its horns and great
size made it look threatening,
the woolly rhinoceros was a
herbivore that grazed on
plants. It lived either a
solitary existence or in very
small groups, much like
rhinoceroses do today.

The front horn of the
woolly rhinoceros was
3 ft (1 m) long.

The shorter horn
was upright,
between the
eyes.

The huge front horn was
probably used to clear
snow, attract mates, and
protect against attack.

The horns were
made of keratin, the
same protein found
in hair and nails.

RHINO REMAINS
The preserved skeletons of woolly
rhinoceroses reveal their vast size, broad rib cage, and short limbs. One,
discovered in 2015, was named Sasha by Russian scientists. Tests on her
teeth revealed she was seven months old when she died and much bigger
than rhinos of the same age today. Experts believe this species died out
about 10,000 years ago as a result of human hunters and climate change
affecting their habitat and availability of food.

Tough skin
covered the
woolly rhino.

The massive body generated heat to keep the rhino warm.

Short, stocky legs supported the woolly rhino's great weight.

The scimitar cat's slim build and flexible spine may have helped it to take big strides.

The lightweight body was similar in size to a lion.

The scimitar cat may have run at speeds of up to 55 mph (90 kph).

Scimitar cats had shorter tails than most modern cats.

FAST FELINE

The athletic build of the scimitar cat can be seen in this computer-generated image. Long legs and razor-sharp teeth were a deadly combination. This successful predator chased young mammoths at high speed across the icy plains and grasslands.

Scimitar cats had small claws that couldn't fully retract.

WEIGHT
Up to 550 lb (230 kg)

The serrated canine teeth were used to stab prey and slice flesh.

Strong jaws helped the scimitar cat to grip prey.

COOL CATS

The fiercest felines walked the Earth during the ice age millions of years ago. Though they had much in common with today's cats, genetic studies show that they are not their direct ancestors. These ferocious predators are sometimes called saber-toothed cats because their huge, curved canine teeth looked like swords.

SCIMITAR SKELETONS

More than 30 fossilized skeletons of scimitar cats were discovered in Friesenhahn Cave in Texas. They show it had a flexible spine and slimline bones suited to high-speed running over short distances. The strong, broad shoulders show it had the strength to carry large prey in its mouth, perhaps to hide it from scavengers. This species died out about 11,000 years ago, when its larger prey also died out.

As in most deer, the
antlers were shed and
regrown every year.

Strong neck muscles
supported the
mighty antlers.

WEIGHT
Up to 1,500 lb (700 kg)

Antlers consisted of bone and used to fight other males.

The amazing antlers of Megaloceros were up to 12 ft (3.5 m) across.

The antlers were used to craft tools.

BIG GAME

The prehistoric plains were dominated by giant deer. These huge, hoofed herbivores lived alongside woolly mammoths and woolly rhinos. All of them were big-game targets for human hunters who played a part in their extinction. Although the giant deer died out during the last ice age, fossils reveal they shared many characteristics with their much smaller modern relatives.

Thick fur covering the body provided warmth and protection.

IRISH ELK

The largest ice-age deer was the Irish Elk, also known as Megaloceros (meaning "great horn"). This computer-generated reconstruction shows the Irish Elk in all its glory. With great antlers and a heavyweight body, it roamed most of the northern continents and was among the largest deer ever known.

SIBERIAN SPECIMENS

Fossils of Megaloceros have helped scientists learn more about when and why this species disappeared. The most recent examples from Siberia are 7,000 years old. The large skeleton and huge antlers—which each weighed up to 44 lb (20 kg)—suggest it may have been slow on its feet and an easy target for hunters. Climate change contributed to their extinction by changing their habitat.

Cave bears had small
eyes and poor vision.

Powerful shoulders and
forelimbs supported the
weighty body.

Coarse fur covered the
body completely.

A large nose
provided a good
sense of smell.

The size, shape,
and structure of
the teeth reveal
that cave bears
mostly ate plants
and fruit.

Cave bears had
wider heads than
modern bears.

BEAR BONES

The fossilized remains of cave bears reveal teeth
evolved for a vegetarian diet. However, the ice
age restricted the growth of plants, so food was
scarce. As human hunters moved into caves, the
hibernation options for bears became limited.
This probably led to their gradual extinction
25,000 years ago. Skeletons show the closest
living relative of cave bears today is the
American brown bear.

LENGTH
Up to 11½ ft (3.5 m)

WEIGHT
Up to 1 ton

Fat stores on the body were used up during hibernation.

CAVE CREATURES

Caves provided safe shelter from the freezing temperatures of the last Ice Age. However, humans did not always get there first. Cave bears are named after these natural dwelling places where they hibernated during the coldest months of the year. The preserved remains of more than 100,000 bears have been found in limestone caves across Europe.

Cave bears were twice the height of an adult human.

BEAR NECESSITIES

Despite their fearsome size, cave bears were probably mainly vegetarian and survived by eating fruit and plants. Their furry coats kept them warm while foraging for food. They did not seek shelter for most of the year and only used caves for the deep sleep of winter hibernation.

ANIMAL EVOLUTION

The mammoths that roamed the tundra during the last ice age were better adapted to cope with the cold than the smaller elephants alive today. Mammoths and modern elephants have both descended from the same ancestor, becoming different through a process called evolution. Bigger and hairier mammoths were more likely to survive their colder climate, and passed these characteristics on to future generations.

A warming climate may have driven ice-age animals such as mammoths to extinction. Modern climate change is likely to do the same.

WARMING CLIMATE

!

The steppe mammoth was adapted to life on the plains of northern Asia and had short hair.

The huge steppe mammoth stood 13 ft (4 m) tall at the shoulder. It lived from 600,000 to 370,000 years ago.

Human hunters may have wiped out the last surviving mammoths.

Long, shaggy hair kept the mammoth warm on the dry grasslands of the far north.

FOSSILS

We know that animals have changed over time because traces of earlier forms have been preserved as fossils. Most fossils are the remains of bones, teeth, or shells that have turned to stone. But in the far north, entire mammoths and other ice-age animals have been found buried in ground that has been frozen for thousands of years. These relics preserve skin, hair, and even the animal's last meal.

EXTINCTION

Over thousands or millions of years, new species evolve to suit changing environments, while others become extinct (die out). As a result, the new species take over from the old ones. But in the modern world, habitat destruction and climate change are happening so rapidly that new species cannot evolve fast enough to replace the ones that disappear. If the polar bear becomes extinct because of melting polar ice, nothing will replace it.

WOOLLY MAMMOTH

The biggest land animal to fully adapt to ice-age conditions was the woolly mammoth, which appeared about 400,000 years ago. It was one of several types of mammoth that evolved from animals similar to modern elephants, developing hairy coats to keep out the ice-age chill. Although smaller than the steppe mammoth, it was better adapted for cold climates.

Woolly mammoths had smaller ears than modern elephants to avoid the risk of frostbite.

ASIAN ELEPHANT

Modern Asian elephants are related to woolly mammoths. They still have some hair like mammoths, especially when they are born.

The tusks of a male could be more than 10 ft (3 m) long.

FROZEN WORLD

Ice dominates the poles, which are covered by vast ice sheets and frozen seas. It also builds up in mountains and creeps down valleys as glaciers. But wherever the ice melts in summer, tough plants can spring up and bring the landscape to life.

THE ARCTIC

At the top of our planet is a freezing-cold habitat: the Arctic. It includes the ice-topped Arctic Ocean, with the North Pole in the middle and a large expanse of treeless, icy land around the sea. Although it's one of the coldest, windiest places on Earth, it is home to many animals, plants, and people.

NIGHT AND DAY

There are just two seasons in the Arctic. In the six months of icy winter, it is dark nearly all day and night. During the warmer six-month summer, it stays light for most or all of the time.

In winter, animals use sea ice as a bridge to travel and find food.

About four million people live in the Arctic. Their ancestors learned to survive in the harsh conditions over many thousands of years.

Polar bears, the Arctic's largest land predators, wait on the ice for seals to surface for air.

Around 10 percent of the world's fresh water is stored in the Greenland ice sheet.

Around March 21, the sun rises at the North Pole. It then circles through the sky every day for six months before setting at the start of winter.

Late summer sea ice in the Arctic has fallen by about 70 percent over the past 40 years. This trend is likely to continue, eventually resulting in ice-free summers.

MELTING SEA ICE

!

Tourist and transport ships share the seas with mammals, sometimes putting them at risk.

The sea ice breaks up into floating chunks in the summer months. These freeze back together in winter.

Seals survive the frosty waters by eating shrimplike krill and fish.

Some animals, like the narwhal, live in Arctic waters all year. They breathe through holes in the ice.

ARCTIC LOCATOR

The Arctic is the northernmost region on Earth. It consists of the Arctic Ocean, smaller surrounding seas, and the most northerly parts of Europe, Asia, and North America.

Every winter, fresh snow falls in the mountains, covering the ice formed from previous snowfalls.

Meltwater lakes may form on the sun-warmed surface of glaciers.

Deep holes called crevasses form as the moving ice cracks.

Glaciers and ice sheets contain about 69 percent of Earth's fresh water.

GLACIERS

When snow builds up on land over many years without melting, it becomes compressed by its own weight into a vast mass of ice—a glacier. Glaciers form in snowcapped mountain ranges and flow slowly downhill, like rivers in slow motion, moving up to 3 ft (1 m) a day. The moving ice scours deep valleys out of the landscape and dumps piles of rubble at the glacier's foot. In Greenland and Antarctica, so much glacial ice has built up over the centuries that these landmasses are buried under sheets of ice hundreds of miles across.

Most of the world's mountain glaciers are shrinking in size due to global warming. If all the world's glaciers and ice sheets melted, sea levels would rise 230 ft (70 m).

SHRINKING GLACIERS

CALVING

The process of calving is the breaking away of chunks of ice from the end of a glacier where it meets a lake or the sea. In a calving event, blocks of ice up to 200 ft (60 m) high crash into the water, causing large waves. In parts of Antarctica, the climate is so cold that the glacial ice remains unbroken for miles out to sea, forming permanent ice shelves that provide habitats for penguins and other animals.

Pulled by the force of gravity, the vast mass of ice flows slowly downhill, creaking loudly as it moves.

A lake or an ocean lies at the end of a calving glacier.

Chunks of ice at the edge of the glacier break off and drift away as icebergs.

GLACIAL FEATURES

MOULINS
Meltwater on flat areas of a large glacier gushes into deep shafts called moulins. The water may flow all the way to the glacier's base, wetting it and helping it move.

MEDIAL MORAINES
Where two glaciers meet, mounds of rocky debris swept downhill by the ice build up in dark stripes. These are known as medial moraines.

MELTWATER STREAMS
In summer, surface water builds up to form meltwater streams that flow in a network of channels over the glacier. These streams may pool together to form lakes.

GLACIER CAVES

An underground wonderland of ice-blue caves lies hidden beneath the Mendenhall Glacier in Alaska. This huge expanse of ice first formed about 3,000 years ago and eventually expanded to cover an area of 37 square miles (95 square km). As meltwater flows through crevasses in the great glacier, it sculpts remarkable caves and tunnels in its base. Their vivid blue coloring comes from daylight filtering through the translucent ice.

Unlike caves in rock, glacier caves are temporary structures and are forever changing. They look very different from one year to the next as the flowing water carves out new shapes and as the whole glacier slowly moves downhill. The spectacle brings thousands of visitors flocking to the ice caves of Alaska every year.

Rising temperatures are melting the Mendenhall Glacier at a rapid rate. Ecosystems and wildlife are affected, and the region's largest source of fresh water is reduced.

MELTING GLACIER

THE TUNDRA

Chilly, windy, and covered in snow for most of the year, the tundra is a harsh, treeless habitat. Summertime brings a welcome thaw—colorful wildflowers bloom and birds flock here to feast on swarming insects. Some animals live there all year round, while others migrate to warmer homes in the winter months.

Tundra animals like the muskox use their hooves to dig through snow and find food.

Some animals hibernate, and many birds leave in winter. Others, like the snowy owl, stay and hunt small mammals scurrying through the snow.

Beneath the surface of the ground is a thick layer of frozen soil called permafrost. This stops roots from growing deep, so only small plants can survive in the tundra.

SUMMERS AND SNOW

About 10 percent of Earth's land surface is Arctic tundra. When the winter snows finally melt, shrubs, grasses, and moss burst into life. Animals that moved out in the snowy season return. The surface snow and ice melt, making the ground boggy.

THE TUNDRA
Most tundra is found in the far north, around the Arctic.

The summer sun provides just enough heat to warm up and thaw the ground surface.

Birds flock to the tundra during the short summer to breed. In winter, some fly south—the Arctic tern flies all the way to Antarctica.

Thawing permafrost, as a result of rising temperatures, releases methane gas into the air, which contributes to global warming.

THAWING PERMAFROST

!

Summer lasts for just six weeks, but the sun shines for more than 20 hours a day.

By grazing on the tundra, Arctic reindeer help sunlight reach lower-lying plants so they can grow.

Tundra birds, like this Smith's longspur, gobble up beakfuls of bugs and raise their young here.

Plants like Arctic moss grow in low cushions that help them withstand fierce winds.

Small shrubs like the Arctic willow grow well in the tundra's marshy soil.

Plants like bearberry have thick leaves to fight the cold.

LICHEN AND MOSS

Very few plants can survive in the world's coldest habitats, where the ground is frozen solid and roots cannot grow. Lichens and mosses, however, survive by clinging to crevices in rock and can endure months at a time without water or light. They grow at a glacial pace, taking as long as 100 years to grow by only a millimeter.

REINDEER MOSS
Despite the name, reindeer moss is not a moss but a lichen that's common in mountain tundra and the forests of the taiga. It is a favorite food of reindeer, which use their hooves to dig through snow in winter to find it.

SUNBURST LICHEN
A lichen is not a plant but a kind of fungus containing microscopic, plantlike organisms that photosynthesize (make food from the energy in light). The sunburst lichen is named for the bright orange sunscreen it produces to shield itself from ultraviolet rays in sunlight.

ARCTIC KIDNEY LICHEN
This large, leaflike lichen thrives in Alaska and Canada, where it provides food for grazing animals. Some of Alaska's indigenous people also ate it, boiling it and then serving it with crushed fish eggs.

MAP LICHEN

Map lichen grows in mountainous regions where the air is fresh and is also a familiar sight on Antarctica's rocky coast. It grows in a patchwork of green patches fringed by black borders, like countries on a world map.

ANTARCTIC MOSS

During Antarctica's brief summer, some parts of the coast turn green as snow melts and the moss hidden below springs back to life. It almost never rains in Antarctica, but moss gets all the water it needs from melting snow.

FIRE MOSS

Fire moss grows in green cushions with vibrant red shoots. This tough survivor can be found all over the world, from cracks in pavements to coastal sand dunes and the rocky slopes of Antarctica.

POLAR PLANTS

Only the toughest plants can live in the polar regions. They must be able to grow in half-frozen ground, withstand icy winds, cope with deep snow cover, and survive months of permanent darkness in winter. But when summer brings almost constant daylight, they all burst into bloom at once.

MOSS CAMPION

Like many Arctic plants, this forms low, dense cushions that resist freezing winds, creating a warmer pocket of air within the plant. The flowers bloom first on its sunny south side, so it is sometimes called the compass plant.

ANTARCTIC HAIRGRASS

Found further south than any other flowering plant, Antarctic hairgrass survives by taking root in rocky crevices on sunny slopes that are sheltered from the worst of the wind.

PASQUEFLOWER

Ranging from purple to white, pasqueflowers grow on slender stems from a clump of low-growing leaves. The entire plant is covered in silky hairs that prevent water loss in strong winds.

ARCTIC POPPY

This yellow poppy can grow on the most barren tundra by rooting in cracks in the rock. It has flowers shaped like satellite dishes that move to follow the sun, focusing its warmth on the developing seeds at the center of each flower.

COTTON GRASS

In the short Arctic summer, large areas of drab tundra swamp are transformed as cotton grass produces its fluffy white seed heads. As these break up, each seed is swept into the air like thistledown, and carried off to a new site.

ARCTIC WILLOW

Most willows are tall trees. But on the northern tundra, Arctic willow rarely reaches 10 in (25 cm) tall—growing so slowly that it may be more than 200 years old. It lives further north than any other woody plant.

BEARBERRY

This Arctic relative of heather grows in northern forests and nearby tundra, forming low shrubs with small leaves that often turn red in fall. Its juicy berries are a favorite food of brown bears.

ARCTIC PEARLWORT

This is one of just two flowering plants that grow in Antarctica (the other is Antarctic hairgrass). Growing to only 2 in (5 cm) tall to keep out of the bitter polar wind, it forms a dense cushion covered with flowers.

PURPLE SAXIFRAGE

As soon as patches of Arctic snow start to melt in spring, purple saxifrage plants burst into flower. Eventually they form carpets of purple, which survive until the snow starts falling at the onset of another winter.

THE TAIGA

South of the frozen tundra, a vast forest region called the taiga stretches in a wide band across North America, Europe, and Asia. Long, dark winters make it bitterly cold here for much of the year. In summer, however, the snow disappears and the days are longer, bringing milder weather.

With a quarter of all trees on Earth, the taiga releases more oxygen than the tropical rain forests.

The hooded crow feeds on seeds, insects, eggs, and dead animals.

The crossbill's unusual crossed beak tips help it pry open pine cones and reach the seeds inside with its tongue.

Pools of water form when the permafrost melts, attracting swarms of buzzing flies and mosquitoes.

Animals like the Siberian musk deer chew on lichen, small bushes, and conifers.

Conifer trees have needle-shaped leaves that can withstand freezing winds and heavy snow.

Some animals, like the European brown bear, hibernate during the long winter to escape the cold and because food is scarce.

THE TAIGA

The taiga forms a ring around the top of the Northern Hemisphere, covering 11.5 percent of Earth's land, including much of Canada, Scandinavia, and Russia.

The black stork flies north from Africa and southern Asia to spend summers in the taiga.

The branches of conifer trees are shaped to let snow slide off easily.

As well as being vulnerable to global warming, taiga trees are sensitive to atmospheric pollution, such as acid rain—and take a very long time to regenerate.

POLLUTION
!

EVERGREEN FORESTS

Unlike the broad-leaved trees that thrive in warmer climates, the conifer trees in the taiga keep their leaves all year. During winter, when the ground freezes, the trees cannot absorb water from the soil. However, their thin leaves have a thick, waxy coating that prevents them from losing moisture.

Seeds in pine cones provide a rich food supply. Some animals store them for winter.

Thick fur coats, an acute sense of smell, and cooperative hunting help packs of wolves survive in the taiga.

In summer, flocks of birds like the Siberian thrush migrate to the taiga to nest and feast on insects and berries.

Low bushes and ferns grow under the canopy of trees.

LIGHT SHOW

The aurora borealis, or northern lights, is one of nature's most spectacular shows. Its glowing patterns can often be seen in the night sky in some of the most northerly parts of the world during winter and spring. This is the result of charged particles from the Sun colliding with gases in Earth's atmosphere. The aurora's colors depend on the type of gases the solar particles are interacting with.

The dazzling display has captivated onlookers since ancient times and inspired many myths. Vikings saw the lights as the reflected shields of their female warriors, while the Inuit believed they were torches held by ravens lighting the way to heaven. Red lights were considered a terrifying warning of war or plague in medieval Europe. Italian physicist and astronomer Galileo Galilei called the northern lights "aurora borealis" after Aurora, the Roman goddess of dawn, and Boreas, the Greek god of the north wind.

▲ A colony of penguins in Antarctica bathes in the glow of the southern lights, or aurora australis.

MOUNTAINS

Life changes the higher you climb up a mountain. In the leafy forests that blanket the lower slopes of the Himalayas, the climate is warm. But higher up, it gets colder and windier, and forests give way to meadows and rocky slopes. The peaks of many mountains are clad in snow and ice year round—a challenge for the animals and plants that live there.

Birds of prey such as the bearded vulture soar high in the mountains to scan the terrain below for food.

Global warming threatens the flow of rivers that rely on meltwater from mountain snow and ice, while deforestation is a threat to forest animals at lower altitude.

MELTWATER

!

Grasses, insects, and small mammals provide food for the Himalayan brown bear during summer trips to high mountain areas.

At heights of over 26,250 ft (8,000 m), the air is too thin for humans, but birds such as bar-headed geese can survive.

The Himalayan jumping spider is one of the highest-living animals on Earth. It sits on rocks in sunny weather, waiting to pounce on small flies.

MOUNTAINS

Mountain ranges form when rocks push up as Earth's surface plates move. Some of the most famous are the Andes in South America, the Rockies in North America, the Alps in Europe, and the Himalayas in Asia.

At 29,029 ft (8,848 m) tall, Mount Everest is the highest peak, and the loftiest habitat, on Earth.

Mountain goats such as the Himalayan tahr have hooves with a rubbery base to grip smooth rocks as they climb.

HIMALAYAS

The Himalayan mountains stretch across Asia, covering parts of China, India, Nepal, and Bhutan. They include ten of the world's 14 highest peaks and hold the world's third-largest reserve of snow and ice after the poles. The mountain range is so large that it blocks the path of rain-bearing weather systems, making the land to its south green and lush but casting a "rain shadow" over the arid grasslands and deserts to the north.

When deep piles of fresh snow settle on older snow or on ice, it can become unstable and slide off—causing an avalanche.

The snow leopard is an expert climber, able to bound silently up treacherous slopes while stalking wild sheep and mountain goats. It has long, luxurious fur and a heavy, very furry tail that it uses for balance while climbing and as a wraparound blanket when sleeping.

ICE

When water turns to ice, it can create some spectacular effects. This is partly because water becomes crystalline as it freezes, forming intricate shapes such as snowflakes. Very cold conditions can make water vapor carried in the air turn directly to ice, and when this freezes onto solid objects, it builds up into beautiful structures made of glittering ice.

Severe frost can become so heavy that it pulls down trees and power cables.

SERACS
Where mountain glaciers tumble over rocky ledges, they split into huge, house-sized blocks called seracs. Divided by deep crevasses, they are dangerously unstable, and falling seracs have killed many climbers.

SNOWFLAKE
At high altitudes, water droplets in clouds freeze to form tiny, six-sided ice crystals. These grow bit-by-bit as more water freezes onto them, forming six-pointed snowflakes, each with its own unique shape.

ICE STACKING
Very cold air makes seas and lakes freeze over at the surface. The ice drifts with the winds and currents, and if it runs into a rocky shore, it often cracks into plates that pile up like stacks of broken glass.

RIME ICE

Tiny water droplets in the air can be chilled below their normal freezing point. If they contact a cold object, such as a tree, they freeze onto it instantly yet remain liquid, forming a type of frost called rime ice that turns every twig into an ice sculpture. This effect is also called freezing fog.

PENITENTES

In high, cold mountains with dry climates, slow evaporation from ancient snowfields creates blades and spires of hardened snow called penitentes. They are particularly common in the South American Andes.

HAIR ICE

Ice forming in rotting wood can grow out of the wood as fine strands that look like snow-white hair. The process is not fully understood, but it is connected with a fungus living in the decaying timber.

FROST FLOWERS

A sudden chill at night can freeze the watery sap in plants so it expands and bursts out in thin, petallike sheets of ice called frost flowers. They are very delicate and soon melted by the sun.

HOAR FROST

On clear winter nights, heat is soon lost from the land, and solid objects are chilled to below the freezing point of water. Any water vapor in the air freezes onto them, forming the white crystals of hoar frost.

NEEDLE ICE

Water moving through cold ground can seep to the surface and freeze on contact with very cold air. As the water pushes upward, ice may form and grow into very thin, needlelike columns.

ANTARCTICA

Nowhere on Earth is less hospitable to life than Antarctica—the coldest, driest, darkest, and windiest continent on Earth. Antarctica is nearly twice the size of Australia but 98 percent of its land is buried under ice sheets up to 1.2 miles (2 km) deep. In winter, the sea around it freezes too, doubling the area covered by ice. Despite the brutal climate, Antarctica is home to many kinds of animals, nearly all of which live around the coast and depend on the sea for food.

By riding on the winds that blow around Antarctica, albatrosses can stay airborne for hours without flapping.

The orca, or killer whale, is one of ten whale species found in the Southern Ocean that surrounds Antarctica. It preys on seals and other whales.

Antarctica's ice flows from land to sea, but very slowly. It takes 50,000 years for a snowflake to travel from the South Pole to the ocean.

ANTARCTIC MAMMALS

The only land-living mammals in Antarctica are seals, most of which live not on the mainland but on ice or on the small islands around Antarctica, where the weather is milder. Southern elephant seals are the world's largest seals and rely on their great bulk to stay warm.

A male southern elephant seal can weigh around 4 tons—more than a female African elephant.

In 1983 the temperature in part of Antarctica fell to -128.6 °F (-89.2 °C), the lowest ever recorded on Earth.

Antarctica has vast mountain ranges, but they are mostly buried in ice, with only the peaks showing through.

The snow petrel is one of the only animals that has ever been seen at the South Pole.

Scientists believe the West Antarctic Ice Sheet is beginning to melt but the larger East Antarctic Ice Sheet is intact.

MELTING ICE SHEET

!

Emperor penguins can endure temperatures of -40 °F (-40 °C) by huddling together in colonies.

Antarctic terns nest on rocky islets and islands around Antarctica and feed at sea, diving for small fish and shrimp.

Antarctic hairgrass is one of only a handful of plants that can survive in Antarctica. Trees can't grow here because the deep soil is frozen solid.

Plant-like organisms called lichens grow as a thin crust on rocks. Some can take 1,000 years to grow by only 0.4 in (1 cm) in the cold climate.

ANTARCTICA
Earth's southernmost continent, Antarctica lies on the South Pole. The sea around it is called the Southern Ocean.

MOUNT EREBUS

Mount Erebus is the only continually active volcano in Antarctica and the most southerly active volcano on Earth. Standing 12,448 ft (3,794 m) tall, this snow-covered peak dominates the landscape. Erebus has been active for about 1.3 million years and produces frequent small eruptions from the sizzling lava lake in its crater, hurling lots of molten rock into the air. Openings in the sides of the volcano, called fumaroles, release steam and other hot gases, which melt the snow to form incredible ice caves. As the escaping steam hits the cold air, it turns into water that instantly freezes to ice, and this builds up to form strange-looking ice chimneys, or towers.

Mount Erebus is located on Ross Island and was discovered in 1841 by polar explorer James Clark Ross, who named the volcano after one of his expedition ships. In 1908, British explorer Ernest Shackleton visited Ross Island, and five members of his expedition team made the first ascent to the summit of Erebus.

▲ When molten rock in the Earth's crust pushes up through the core of a volcano, a fiery mixture of lava, ash, and steam erupts from the top.

SEA ICE

In winter, air temperatures over polar oceans plunge to well below the freezing point of seawater, which is about 28°F (−2°C). This makes the surface water turn to ice, which gets thicker until rising temperatures make it melt away. Some ice may last for more than one season, especially near the North Pole. Icebergs that drift in polar seas have a quite different origin, being fragments of glaciers that flow off the land.

PACK ICE

Thick ice that drifts with the wind and current is known as pack ice or drift ice. Although up to 4 ft (1.2 m) thick, it is often broken up into separate ice floes by the waves. These slabs of floating ice may be up to 6 miles (10 km) across, but most are far smaller. Ocean currents often push them together and pile them up into stacks of broken ice called pressure ridges.

FRAZIL ICE

When seawater starts to freeze it forms small, floating ice crystals, known as frazil ice. Kept moving by the wind and waves, the crystals clump together but do not form a solid sheet. Instead, they build up in a thin, slushy surface layer that is often described as grease ice.

NILAS ICE

Eventually the separate plates of pancake ice join together in a thin but continuous sheet of nilas ice. The joins are flexible enough to allow the sheet to bend with the waves. As more water freezes onto the ice, it becomes thicker and more rigid, turning to solid pack ice.

PANCAKE ICE

As soupy frazil ice thickens, the crystals freeze onto each other to form small plates of sheet ice. The waves knock these together, crumpling their edges to create pancake ice. Each piece of pancake ice can be up to 10 ft (3 m) across, but is never more than 4 in (10 cm) thick.

MULTIYEAR ICE
Most sea ice melts in summer, but some does not. In the Arctic, pack ice that drifts over the region around the North Pole gets thicker and thicker. It reaches 13 ft (4 m) thick in places, with 66-ft- (20-m-) deep pressure ridges. But even this eventually melts away when it drifts south again.

LEADS
Drifting pack ice can be pulled apart by the currents as well as pushed together. Cracks in the ice widen into long stretches of open water called leads. These can be vital for air-breathing whales, seals, and seabirds that dive under the ice, and can even be used by ships.

FAST ICE
Thick sea ice that is attached to the shore is called fast ice. It is separated from the drifting pack ice by a band of ice floes. Rising and falling tides can make the floating ice crack up near the shore, but the movement is so slow that the cracks keep freezing up again.

ICE SHELVES

Antarctica is home to gigantic floating ice shelves. They form where sheets of thick ice spill out over the ocean. The landward side is connected to the ice sheet on land and is fed by a continuous flow of ice toward the sea.

The Ross Ice Shelf, the largest of all, is about the same size as Spain. Up to 90 percent of the floating ice lies below the surface of the water. The front edge forms a sheer cliff face, which is about 370 miles (600 km) long and towers up to 164 ft (50 m) above the Ross Sea. Great chunks of ice can break away (calve) and form icebergs. The Ross Ice Shelf takes its name from British explorer James Clark Ross who was the first to set eyes on this spectacular feature in 1841. It has since served as a gateway for many of the Antarctic's celebrated expeditions.

▲ Antarctic ice shelves are scoured by strong winds that create patterns of ridges and channels, known as sastrugi, in the surface.

ICEBERGS

During the last ice age, one-third of Earth was under ice. Most of the ice has now melted away, and what remains is largely found at the poles. This is where huge chunks of freshwater ice break away from glaciers and ice shelves before floating into the world's oceans as icebergs.

Only 10 percent of an iceberg is visible above water.

Icebergs are at least 16 ft (5 m) wide but can be massive floating islands hundreds of miles long.

The bright blue tinge of some icebergs comes from densely packed ice without any air bubbles.

MOVING MOUNTAINS

Icebergs break away in a process called calving. Many break off from the great glaciers of Greenland. More than 40,000 form here every year, while thousands more are calved from the ice shelves in Antarctica.

A ship can sink if the impact of hitting an iceberg rips a large-enough hole in its hull.

Icebergs usually appear white because of air bubbles trapped inside the ice.

Growlers are very small icebergs that are hard to spot and hazardous to ships.

Some icebergs have a striped or banded appearance.

Ice above the water surface will usually melt more slowly than ice underwater.

ICEBERG TYPES

TABULAR OR FLAT-TOPPED
The largest icebergs, which have usually broken off the ice shelves in Antarctica, have a flat-topped shape and steep sides. They may float 200 ft (60 m) above the surface.

DOMED
The main part of this iceberg is tabular, but it becomes rounder near the top and leads into a distinctive dome.

PINNACLE
Some icebergs have spires and look similar to mountain peaks. Pinnacle icebergs have at least one tall spire, but many have multiple spires.

SOUTH GEORGIA

In the chilly waters of the Southern Ocean around Antarctica lies one of the world's most inhospitable islands: South Georgia. This remote British territory, along with the smaller South Sandwich Islands, is a land of spectacular mountains, glaciers, and rocky slopes. The islands have a bitterly cold climate, with strong winds and rain that often falls as snow.

Although there are no permanent human inhabitants, wildlife thrives on South Georgia and the South Sandwich Islands. Millions of birds have established colonies, including king, macaroni, and gentoo penguins, and the skies are full of gulls, petrels, skuas, and terns. The South Georgia pipit and South Georgia pintail are unique to the islands. The clifftops provide a safe haven for nesting albatrosses, while elephant and fur seals gather on the beaches. The first person to set foot on South Georgia was British explorer Captain James Cook, who landed here in 1775 and named the island after King George III.

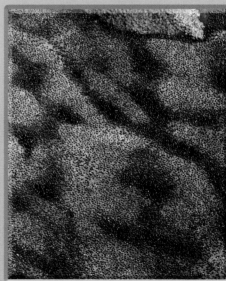

▲ A colony of king penguins and their chicks clustered together for warmth and protection.

ANIMALS ON ICE

No animal could survive in a permanently frozen world. But where the land thaws out each summer, in polar regions or on high mountains, hardy plants can grow and provide food for animals. Meanwhile, polar seas teem with plankton, which support fish, whales, and other marine life.

A dense layer of blubber keeps polar bears warm.

The fur acts as camouflage in the snowy landscape.

The polar bear's fur is thicker than that of any other bear.

LIFE IN THE FREEZER
Polar bear mothers stay with their cubs for more than two years and teach them how to hunt. Ice floes provide a base while searching for seals in the Arctic Ocean. Polar bears are excellent swimmers and can travel for hundreds of miles in the water.

The sharp claws give polar bears excellent grip on the ice.

Cubs stay close to their mothers for protection from predators.

ARCTIC ACE

This record-breaking bear is the world's largest carnivore on land. It is also the biggest and deadliest bear on Earth. Well adapted to the Arctic terrain, the polar bear is accomplished on slippery ice and moves with ease both on land and in water.

Young bears enjoy play fighting, but adult males fight aggressively over food and mates.

The small ears reduce heat loss.

SNOW DENS

In winter, female bears dig dens in the snow to give birth and protect their newborn cubs from the freezing temperatures. The dens are built on land, close to the coast for hunting. Cubs start walking at two months, but continue to spend most of their time in the den and sleep there at night. Staying close together in the shelter helps them survive the coldest months of the year until they are strong enough to trek to the sea ice in spring.

The sensitive nose can smell seals from nearly 1 mile (1.6 km) away.

The polar bear's black skin, only visible on the nose, absorbs the sun's heat.

Polar bears can run at 25 mph (40 kph) and swim at 6 mph (10 kph).

MELTDOWN

Our planet is warming up. Rising temperatures are melting ice at the poles, causing ice sheets to disappear and sea levels to rise. The changes affect animals' habitats, forcing species to move home in search of food, to escape predators, and ultimately to survive.

As sea ice melts, polar bears will be forced back onto land, where they may come into conflict with humans more often.

Polar bears have to swim farther between dwindling ice sheets, using up precious energy.

The ice is melting earlier in spring and forming later in fall, giving polar bears less time to find food.

POLAR PROBLEM

Melting sea ice is a problem for polar bears in the Arctic Ocean. Ice floes are important for them to travel, rest, and hunt. Without these floating bases, the world's biggest bears may starve.

Polar bear numbers are expected to drop two-thirds by the year 2050.

ON THIN ICE

Polar bears are not alone in their fight for survival. Rising temperatures could leave many other vulnerable creatures on thin ice.

RINGED SEALS

Ringed seals are the main prey of polar bears. They build snow shelters on the ice, where they give birth and protect their newborn pups. If temperatures keep rising, their habitat will disappear.

ADÉLIE PENGUINS

Adélie penguin numbers have fallen by more than 80 percent in the last 50 years due to lower numbers of fish and krill in their feeding sites.

ARCTIC FOX

As the weather warms up in the Arctic tundra, the Arctic fox may be left with fewer lemmings and rodents to eat. Meanwhile, a rival predator, the red fox, is encroaching upon its territory.

WINTER WONDERS

Reindeer (known as caribou in North America) can stay warm in winter as blood flowing down the legs transfers its heat to blood flowing up, so body warmth is retained and not lost. They have large, crescent-shaped hooves that act like snowshoes, supporting them on snow or boggy ground. They also use the hooves to dig through snow for food.

The large nose and long snout absorb warmth from exhaled air, helping reindeer stay warm.

In summer, reindeer eyes are golden, but in winter, they change to deep blue, which may improve their vision during the darker days.

PLANT EATERS

During the short northern summer, the Arctic tundra turns green as snow melts and plants spring to life. The carpet of greenery attracts vast numbers of plant-eating mammals, such as reindeer. Traveling in herds of up to 1 million, tundra reindeer spend their life on the move. They migrate north to the tundra for summer and trek hundreds of miles south again every winter.

The reindeer is the only deer species in which both sexes can grow antlers.

A reindeer calf can outrun an Olympic sprinter at 1 day old.

A new pair of antlers grows every year. Growing antlers are covered in a hairy layer of skin called velvet.

A warm, woolly undercoat is covered by a layer of longer, air-filled hairs. These act like a life jacket, helping reindeer float as they swim across rivers.

Habitat loss, unregulated hunting and possibly more blood-sucking mosquitoes due to global warming have led to a 40% drop in wild reindeer numbers in the last 10-25 years.

REINDEER
!

ON THE HOOF

Tundra reindeer migrate farther than any other land mammal on Earth, making round trips up to 3,000 miles (5,000 km) a year in their never-ending search for food. In summer, they head north to coastal plains around the Arctic Ocean to give birth, but here, they are plagued by blood-sucking insects that breed in the marshy tundra, and they can lose up to 1¾ pints (1 liter) of blood a week. To escape the biting pests, they sometimes walk to higher ground, where the wind is too strong for mosquitoes to fly. Here, a herd in Alaska seeks refuge from the insects while resting on ice.

▲ These young Svalbard reindeer must stay close to their mothers for safety. Reindeer calves are fast runners, but many fall prey to gray wolves, wolverines, and lynxes.

The horns have a huge base, the boss, that nearly covers the beast's forehead.

The soft underfur, with fine hairs, keeps the musk ox warm.

The sharp horns are used to threaten and fight rivals.

The lips, nostrils, and eyes are the only parts of the body not covered in thick fur.

LENGTH
Up to 8 ft 3 in (2.5 m)

WEIGHT
Up to 900 lb (400 kg)

CONSERVATION
Least concern

MIGHTY OX

Hardy musk oxen herds have tramped the tundra for more than a quarter of a million years. Their name comes from the musky smell given off by males during the mating season.

TEAM DEFENSE

When predators such as wolves are on the prowl, musk oxen get defensive. They run together to form a tight circle, with pointy horns facing out. Any calves stay safe inside the circle. If that doesn't work, a musk ox may run out with its head lowered to scare predators away.

When male oxen clash horns, the sound can be heard a mile away.

Battling males crash and bash horns up to 20 times during a fight.

Rivals collide at speeds of up to 31 mph (50 kph).

Populations are stable and musk oxen have increased their range in parts of North America, but the long-term effects of global warming are likely to be damaging.

MUSK OX

!

CLASH OF THE TITANS

Ready to rumble? The rut—the annual mating season of large herbivores like deer and musk oxen—involves some of the fiercest battles in the animal world. Every year, males try to impress the females and ward off rival males. Pawing the ground and bashing their horns or antlers, they make their mark and test their opponents. They push, shove, roar, or full-on fight.

LEADERS OF THE PACK

A wolf pack is led by a single pair called the alpha male and alpha female. They are the only members of the pack that breed. The rest of the pack consists mostly of their adult offspring, who share the job of looking after pups.

Most Arctic and tundra wolves are white for camouflage against the snow.

A keen sense of smell is essential to wolves, who find prey by following scent.

WEIGHT
Up to 135 lb (62 kg)
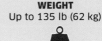

LENGTH
Up to 4.3 ft (1.3 m)
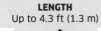

CONSERVATION
Least concern

To reduce heat loss, Arctic wolves have smaller ears than other types of wolves.

Canada's Arctic wolves have no fear of humans and will approach and stalk people who enter their territory.

The members of the pack work together to isolate a single animal from its herd.

Large animals are difficult to overpower, so wolves first chase them to exhaustion, often running for miles.

Muskox are their main prey, but Arctic and tundra wolves also eat reindeer, hares, and lemmings.

The wolves attack the animal from the rear, where they are less likely to be injured.

ICE PACKS

Unlike polar bears, which lead largely solitary lives, Arctic wolves and tundra wolves live and hunt in packs. Living in a group has many advantages. As well as hunting as a team, pack members cooperate to rear their young and to defend their territory from rival packs. Life in the pack is governed by a strict code of conduct, with one dominant pair of wolves in charge of the others.

Arctic wolf numbers are currently stable, but wolves may be persecuted by hunters because of public fears.

ARCTIC WOLF

RUNNING ON ICE

Slippery slopes come with the territory in the world's coldest climates. Arctic animals have special features to withstand the low temperatures and challenging terrain. Whether chasing prey or escaping predators, creatures who live on ice must learn to maintain their speed in order to survive.

The Arctic hare can travel 6 ft (2 m) in a single leap.

The fur consists of a long thick top coat covering a short, dense undercoat.

Male hares stand up on their hind legs to box each other in the fight for females.

FUR BALLS

Arctic hares spend long periods staying still to conserve energy. To stay warm, they make themselves as small as possible, with their ears flat and tail tucked. Only the protective pads of their hind feet touch the cold snow, so the hares can keep warm.

The tough front claws are used to dig down into the snow when searching for plants to eat.

WEIGHT
Up to 15 lb (7 kg)

CONSERVATION
Least concern

Shorter ears than usual for a hare ensure only minimal heat is lost.

HIGH-SPEED HOPPER

The fast-moving Arctic hare uses its long hind legs to cross the icy tundra. A white coat is the perfect camouflage in these snowy surroundings, but it can turn gray or brown if the snow melts.

Eyes positioned on the sides of the head give the hare almost 360-degree vision.

A strong sense of smell helps the hare detect food deep under the snow.

Large, padded hind feet act as snowshoes to stop the hare sinking into the snow.

HERDS OF HARES

Like many creatures, Arctic hares find strength in numbers. Groups of hares can number hundreds or thousands. Traveling together gives them a better chance of spotting predators—before attempting to outrun them at speeds up to 40 mph (60 kph).

THE INVISIBLES

Whether hiding from predators or stalking prey, many Arctic animals depend on camouflage to survive. In winter, many turn pure white to help them blend in with the swirling snow and ice. During the short Arctic summer, when the snow melts, they shed their winter coats and turn gray or black.

FURRY AND FOXY

Able to withstand brutal polar temperatures of -94°F (-70°C), the Arctic fox keeps warm with a fluffy, double-layered coat of winter fur. Most Arctic foxes turn gray in summer but some stay gray all year.

The Arctic Fox's coat has three times as many hairs in winter as in summer.

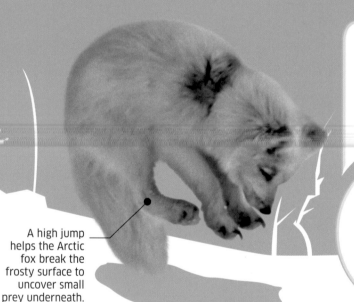

A high jump helps the Arctic fox break the frosty surface to uncover small prey underneath.

Arctic fox numbers are stable across much of the tundra, but some foxes are threatened by disease and pollution.

ARCTIC FOX

!

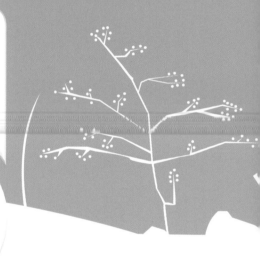

COLOR CHANGERS

ARCTIC HARE
In the far north, Arctic hares are snowy white all year. Hares in southern regions molt into brown coats in summer to blend in with the rocks and plants.

PTARMIGAN
The feathers of birds may change with the season, too. The ptarmigan has pure white feathers in winter. They grow down to their toes to help them cross snowdrifts.

LEAST WEASEL
Color change is linked with the number of daylight hours. Shorter days are a signal for least weasels to start replacing brown hair with bright white fur.

Sensitive hearing helps the fox detect lemmings or other small prey hiding in the snow.

Small ears lose less heat than larger ones.

The eyes are pigmented and shaped to help cut the glare from the ice and snow.

The rounded, small shape helps the fox keep its body heat.

The short snout is the only part of the body not thickly furred.

The Arctic fox can wrap its long, bushy tail around itself like a blanket, tucking in its nose for protection.

The soles of its feet are covered in thick fur to keep its feet warm.

The wolverine's dark, oily fur repels water, so it doesn't get frosty.

Powerful jaws and special molar teeth enable wolverines to rip flesh off carrion that has frozen solid.

WOLVERINE

This ferocious carnivore is famous for its ability to kill animals many times larger than itself, including reindeer floundering in deep snow. Wolverines are related to weasels but are larger and stockier, with a bearlike build. They get much of their food by scavenging from wolf and lynx kills, but they will also attack any live animal they can overpower.

The broad feet have long claws that double as crampons, helping the animal walk on ice.

WEIGHT
Up to 40 lb (18 kg)

CONSERVATION
Least concern

ANIMALS OF THE TAIGA

The vast wilderness of snowy conifer forests that stretches across the northern continents is known as the taiga. Bitterly cold winters and short summers make this a challenging habitat, but many tough animals thrive here, including some of the world's most fierce predators.

Wolverine numbers are dropping, likely due to human encroachment on habitats or illegal hunting in places where these carnivores are thought to attack livestock.

WOLVERINE
!

An acute sense of smell is key when potential prey find cover under snow or earth. Wolverines can dig 20 ft (6 m) deep to uncover burrowing animals.

A wolverine may travel over 19 miles (30 km) a day in its search for food.

FOREST FORAGERS

MOOSE
The moose nibbles on trees, shrubs, and grasses and is the largest animal in the taiga. Its extra-long legs help it move through even the deepest snow.

BOREAL OWL
These birds have super-sensitive hearing and vision. They can see in the dark and can use their ears to pinpoint the location of animals hiding under snow.

SIBERIAN CHIPMUNK
These small, striped squirrels scamper through the forests collecting seeds in their stretchy cheeks. They bury food in fall and hibernate in winter.

The ears are small to minimize loss of heat.

The dense fur grows longer in winter for extra warmth.

LENGTH
Up to 49 in (125 cm)

WEIGHT
Up to 115 lb (52 kg)

CONSERVATION
Vulnerable

87

ALPINE ANIMALS

The snowy peaks of Earth's alpine mountainous regions are as wild as they are beautiful. Animals that live on mountains face freezing temperatures, bitter wind, treacherous rocky slopes, and thin mountain air. Yet many species have learned to survive in these harsh conditions.

Snow leopards growl, hiss, wail, chuff, and even mew—but they cannot roar.

Wide nasal cavities warm the frosty air before it reaches the snow leopard's lungs.

TOP CAT
The snow leopard is well adapted to its home high in the mountains of Asia. Prowling quietly across the rocky terrain, the big cat keeps balance with an oversized tail. Its large paws act like snowshoes to help it walk on snow and ice.

The spotted coat helps the leopard blend into its rocky mountain habitat.

An extra-long tail helps the cat balance as it climbs.

Strong legs power leaps of up to 30 ft (10 m).

The paws are wide with furry soles, giving a good grip on slippery snow.

LIFE AT THE TOP

HIMALAYAN JUMPING SPIDER
Perhaps the animal with the highest address in the world, this eight-eyed spider has been found 20,000 ft (6 km) up a mountain and gobbles up insects blown from below.

VICUNA
This relative of the llama lives high in the Andes. It has an unusually large heart to help it survive in the oxygen-poor air. A dense coat keeps it warm in the icy temperatures.

ANDEAN CONDOR
Soaring on mountain air currents, this enormous vulture is one of the world's largest flying birds. It has excellent vision and uses its high vantage point to spot carcasses from a great distance.

REGION/HABITAT	LENGTH	WEIGHT	CONSERVATION
Arctic	Up to 5.2 ft (1.6 m)	Up to 200 lbs (90 kg)	Least concern

POLAR PREY

Plant life is thin on the ground in polar habitats, so most animals depend on the flesh of other creatures to survive. The tiny animals of the plankton are food for filter-feeders such as baleen whales, and for fish, which are preyed on by bigger animals such as seals. Fish, in turn, are prey to top predators such as killer whales and polar bears.

The ringed seal depends on sea ice to rest on and when raising its pups. As the climate warms and ice melts, its habitat is likely to shrink.

MELTING ICE

SNOW CAVE
Ringed seal mothers hide their pups in snow caves that they dig out on sea ice, with a hole in the ice to come and go. Although hidden from sight, these dens can be smelled by polar bears, which use their great weight to smash through the roof.

Pups have white, woolly fur, which provides warmth and camouflage in snow.

Breathing hole

Ringed seals use the claws on their front flippers to dig breathing holes in floating ice.

When danger threatens, ringed seals slide off their ice floes or dive through their breathing holes into the water.

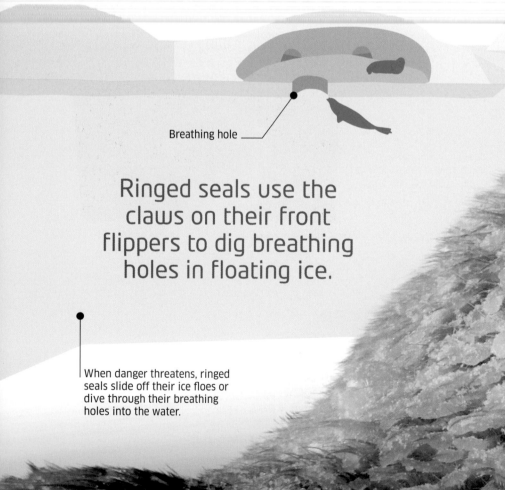

MORE POLAR PREY

COLLARED LEMMING
This rodent cuts and stores grasses so it has a year-round supply of food. It hides under the snow, but many are caught by foxes, weasels, owls, and even wolves.

TUNDRA VOLE
When this mouselike mammal senses danger in its tundra habitat, it scampers down a maze of twisting tunnels to make a speedy escape.

KRILL
These shrimplike animals are about the size of a human thumb and multiply in vast numbers in polar seas. They are food for many animals from penguins to whales.

As a seal grows up, its woolly fur is replaced by more dense, streamlined fur, and a layer of insulating blubber develops under its skin.

The large eyes provide excellent vision in the gloomy light under the ice.

SEAL PUP
Ringed seal pups spend their first six weeks of life hiding in their snow den or practicing swimming. They spend about half their time in the water and can hold their breath for ten minutes at a time.

REGION/HABITAT
Arctic

LENGTH
Up to 28 in (70 cm)

WEIGHT
Up to 6½ lb (3 kg)

90

FEATHERED GIANTS

The coldest places on Earth are home to some of the world's largest birds of prey. These skilled hunters use their sharp eyesight to spot prey from miles away. Dense feathers provide the warmth necessary to thrive in these remote locations.

Forward-facing eyes give snowy owls a wide view, helping them judge distances accurately.

Flexible joints in the neck allow snowy owls to twist their heads to look around.

Hovering in mid-air enables the snowy owl to spot signs of movement on the ground.

The sharp beak is used to grip and butcher prey.

The snowy owl population is declining rapidly as a result of hunting, aeroplane strikes, and collisions with vehicles. As global temperatures rise and lemming populations decline, their numbers may fall further.

Female snowy owls have black flecks on their feathers, while males are almost completely white.

The snowy owl's dense plumage makes it one of the heaviest owls in North America.

SNOWY OWL
!

FINE FEATHERS

Most owls hunt under cover of night, but snowy owls living in the Arctic are camouflaged to hunt by day. A wind-proof outer layer of feathers covers a soft, downy inner layer.

Soft feathers on the top of the wings muffle sound, allowing owls to swoop on prey silently.

The whopping wingspan of a snowy owl can exceed 5 ft (1.5 m).

The feet are covered in fluffy feathers to keep them warm.

SWOOPING KILLERS

SOUTHERN GIANT PETREL
This huge Antarctic bird is an aggressive attacker that also scavenges on dead seals and penguins. Spitting a foul-smelling substance at predators has earned it the nickname "stinker."

GYRFALCON
The world's largest falcon is a ruthless hunter in its Arctic home. Gyrfalcons usually seize rodents and hares on the ground, but occasionally launch an aerial attack by dropping on prey from above.

STELLER'S SEA EAGLE
With a wingspan of 8 ft (2.5 m) and a body weight of up to 20 lb (9 kg), this powerfully built Russian eagle snatches fish from the water and has the fat reserves to survive freezing temperatures.

LIFE ON THE WING

The wandering albatross spends most of its life in the air, landing only to feed or breed. They may even sleep while flying. Gliding almost effortlessly on its colossal wings, an albatross can cover 75,000 miles (120,000 km) a year as it cruises over the windswept Southern Ocean in search of food. Wandering albatrosses live for around 50 years and mate with the same partner for life.

With a wingspan of up to 11 ft (3.5 m), the wandering albatross has the longest wings of any bird. It uses the long wings to catch the wind, allowing it to glide for hours at a time without flapping.

PARENTING

Albatrosses breed on islands in the Southern Ocean, building mud nests on high ground where they can take to the air simply by extending their wings to catch the wind. They raise a single chick every two years, and the two parents take turns sitting on the nest while the other partner searches for food. To feed the chick, they regurgitate a rich stomach oil made from half-digested fish, squid, and krill.

Webbed feet allow the adult albatrosses to swim like ducks and rest in the sea after feeding. They can dive up to 3 ft (1 m) deep but prefer to catch surface fish by swooping close to the water.

WEIGHT
Up to 26 lbs (12 kg)

WEIGHT
Up to 26 lbs (12 kg)

CONSERVATION
Vulnerable

An albatross can travel 6,000 miles (10,000 km) in a single journey.

In summer the islands around Antarctica become a theater for the spectacular courtship dances of young albatrosses that gather on the islands to find mates.

Wandering albatrosses are threatened by longline fishing, which can trap birds as they try to pick fish from baited hooks.

LIFELONG PARTNERS

Wandering albatrosses don't find mates until at least 10 years old, but then stay together for life. Each time they meet, the pair cements their bond by calling, tapping beaks, and preening each other. They spend 11 weeks incubating their single egg and another 10 months feeding the growing chick.

Albatrosses get rid of salt from their nostrils, allowing them to drink seawater.

WANDERING ALBATROSS

!

MEGA MIGRATORS

Summertime in the Arctic sees an abundance of animals arriving to take advantage of the feeding and breeding conditions. Come winter, the temperature plummets, so they travel south by air, sea, or land to reach warmer places. Some of these migrators cover record-breaking distances on their epic journeys.

FREQUENT FLIER

About one-third of the world's birds migrate, and the Arctic tern has the longest migration of them all. Every year, this seabird leaves the icy winter of the Arctic, traveling to Antarctica.

Pin-sharp vision helps the Arctic tern spot fish from a distance.

The beak has a sharp tip to catch slippery fish.

A slimline body and hollow bones help this lightweight bird make its long-distance flight.

GRACEFUL GLIDERS

Also known as sea swallows, Arctic terns appear to fly effortlessly over the ocean. By harnessing the power of the wind beneath their wings, they glide long distances without flapping, conserving precious energy. They can also hover in one spot to look for prey, before dive-bombing into the waves at speed. Their long route between the poles is not always the same because the birds may change direction to avoid bad weather or to follow large shoals of fish.

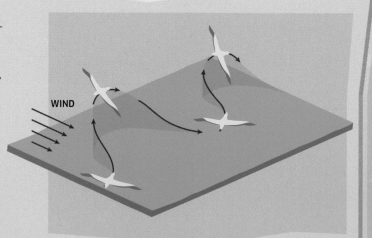

WIND

Long wings span up to 33 in (85 cm) in total.

The wings are stationary when the tern is gliding.

The Arctic tern's astonishing return trip between the poles is 44,000 miles (70,000 km) long.

Webbed feet and short legs are tucked in to create a streamlined shape.

The tail feathers spread out during fast flight but are brought together before diving into the sea.

LONG-DISTANCE TRAVELERS

HUNGRY HUMPBACKS
Humpback whales cover 3,000 miles (5,000 km) annually—one of the longest mammal migrations on Earth. Each summer they leave the icy North Pacific to feast on krill in the warmer tropical waters.

ROAMING REINDEER
The freezing Arctic winters make more than a million caribou migrate in search of warmer temperatures and plentiful food. Their hardworking hooves can cover 1,600 miles (2,575 km) in a year.

SOARING SHEARWATERS
Millions of short-tailed shearwaters leave their Australian homelands every year and fly to the Aleutian Islands of Alaska. This migration over a distance of 9,000 miles (15,000 km) takes about six weeks.

MARCH OF THE PENGUINS
During the month of March, entire colonies of emperor penguins in Antarctica follow a treacherous route over the ice and snow to reach their breeding grounds up to 75 miles (120 km) away.

BLACK-LEGGED KITTIWAKE
This gull breeds in big, noisy colonies on sheer cliffs in and near the Arctic. Each pair nests on a tiny ledge, just wide enough for one or two chicks.

BRÜNNICH'S GUILLEMOT
Brünnich's guillemots can find their eggs and chicks in vast colonies of over a million adults.

NORTHERN FULMAR
Although it looks like a gull, the northern fulmar is more closely related to albatrosses. Fulmars can defend themselves by spraying liquid from their stomach at an attacker.

SNOWY OWL
Widespread around the Arctic, snowy owls often hunt small mammals such as mice by listening for their squeaks and rustles beneath the snow.

SNOWY SHEATHBILL
This is the only Antarctic bird that is not a type of seabird. It survives on icy shores by scavenging scraps from seal and penguin colonies.

ANTARCTIC SHAG
Shags are seabirds that hunt underwater, propelled by their large webbed feet. This species nests on the rocky Antarctic Peninsula and nearby islands.

COMMON EIDER
This sea duck lives all around the Arctic. It lines its nest with soft down feathers, which are traditionally harvested for making eiderdown quilts.

NORTHERN ROCKHOPPER PENGUIN
The rockhopper is one of the most aggressive of all penguins and catches prey from the cold but food-rich ocean.

WANDERING ALBATROSS
A huge, 10-ft (3-m) wingspan allows the wandering albatross to soar over the windswept Southern Ocean for hours without a single wingbeat.

ARCTIC TERN
After breeding in the Arctic, this sleek seabird flies around the world to feed in Antarctic waters—a trip of more than 12,000 miles (19,000 km).

POLAR BIRDS

Many birds thrive in icy polar regions, especially in summer, when the endless daylight gives them ample time to find food for their young. Some leave to spend the winter in warmer places, but a few stay all year.

ARCTIC REDPOLL
This small finch feeds mainly on tree seeds. It nests on the ground among rocks or on low trees, moving south to escape the Arctic winter.

ATLANTIC PUFFIN
The Atlantic puffin can carry a dozen fish at a time in its colorful bill. It hunts underwater, swimming with its wings.

LITTLE AUK
The little auk is found throughout the Arctic. It preys on tiny shrimplike animals, eating thousands each day.

ANTARCTIC SKUA
Although powerful enough to kill a penguin chick, the gull-like Antarctic skua relies more on piracy, stealing food from other seabirds in midair.

ROCK PTARMIGAN
A type of grouse, the rock ptarmigan lives in the Arctic on treeless tundra and mountains. In winter, it turns white for camouflage in the snow.

SNOW GOOSE
In spring, millions of snow geese fly north from the US to breed on the tundra of Arctic Canada. They may fly 3,100 miles (5,000 km) or more.

Hundreds of sensitive whiskers help walruses find food in murky water on the seabed.

GREAT GATHERINGS

Many animals around the world gather in groups to feed, breed, sleep, or migrate. This can be a good way to find mates, scare off predators, target prey, and protect young. In the coldest climates, large groups of animals also huddle together to keep warm and survive the winter.

Walruses use their tusks to help them climb out of the water onto ice.

HAULING OUT

When the Arctic ice begins to melt in summer, large groups of walruses seek shelter on land. This is called "hauling out," and it can be a dangerous move. Predatory polar bears and noisy vehicles can scare the walruses, which rush into the sea for safety. Many die in the sudden stampede and calves are particularly vulnerable.

Hunting, pollution, and human disturbance are taking their toll on walruses, but shrinking sea ice – used for pupping and haul-outs – poses a bigger threat.

WALRUS

!

WEIGHTY WALRUS

The walrus is among the mightiest marine mammals and is easily recognizable by its huge, blubbery body and long tusks. These strong swimmers dive deep to hunt shellfish on the ocean floor, often resting on sea ice between dives.

The gray skin turns pink in warm weather as blood rushes to the surface to help the walrus cool down.

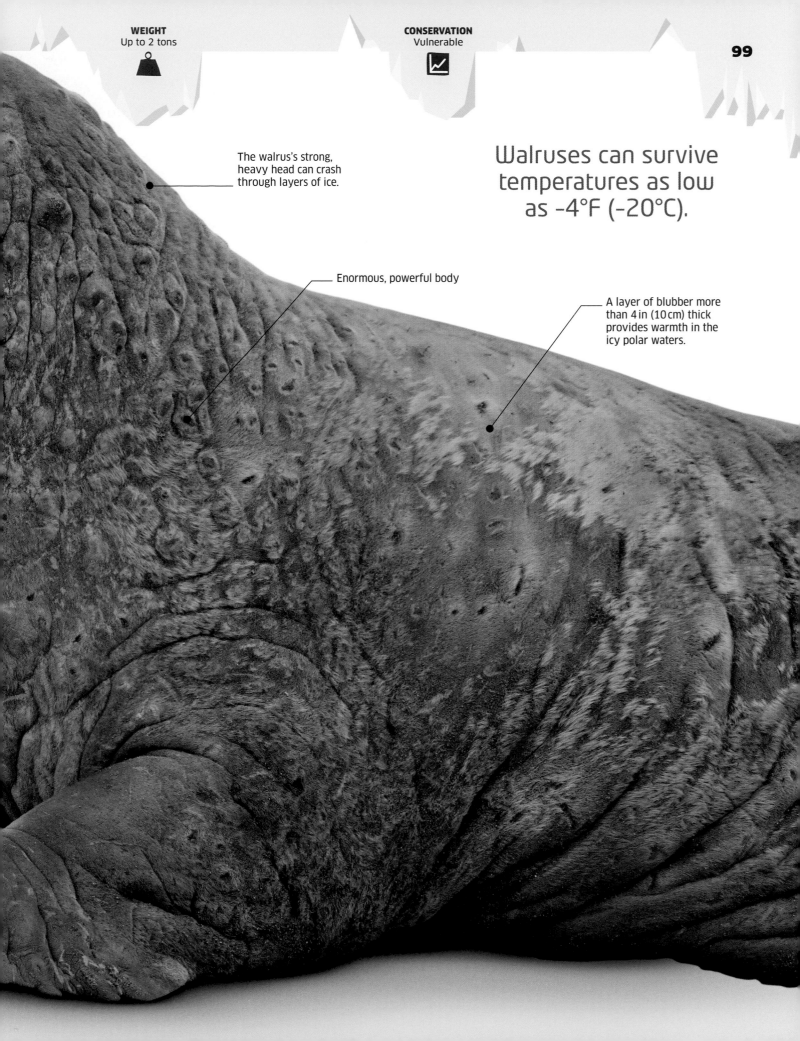

WEIGHT
Up to 2 tons

CONSERVATION
Vulnerable

The walrus's strong, heavy head can crash through layers of ice.

Enormous, powerful body

A layer of blubber more than 4 in (10 cm) thick provides warmth in the icy polar waters.

Walruses can survive temperatures as low as –4°F (–20°C).

WALRUS RETREAT

Ice floes provide a safe haven for Atlantic walruses and their young. They can rest on the ice in the sunshine without fear of predators or people coming too close. These floating platforms are also the perfect base from which to dive into the waters below and forage for seafood. As the floes move about, the walruses can explore new underwater hunting areas.

In every herd of walruses, there is a clear hierarchy. The biggest male with the longest tusks and the most aggressive attitude dominates the group. Smaller males with lesser or damaged tusks must give way to the leader. Tusks are used as weapons when mature males fight in the mating season, and this is evident in the many scars that mark their thick hides.

▲ This bull Atlantic walrus has dived to the seabed to search for clams off the coast of Greenland.

102

REGION/HABITAT
Subantarctic

HEIGHT
Up to 39 in (100 cm)

WEIGHT
Up to 40 lb (18 kg)

SLICK SWIMMERS

Penguins are the ultimate ocean birds, specialized for hunting underwater for fish, squid, and shrimplike krill. Though clumsy on land and unable to fly, they are agile and fast in the water. Penguins can also endure the coldest weather on Earth.

Too short for flight, penguin wings are the ideal size and shape for propelling the bird underwater.

The long, sharp bill is ideal for seizing fast-swimming fish and squid.

A penguin's eyes have lenses that are specially adapted to see clearly both in air and in water.

PENGUIN FEATHERS

Penguins have a short but very dense layer of feathers that makes them streamlined in the water but also helps them stay warm on land. Stiff outer feathers keep the wind out, and down feathers beneath trap air for insulation. The air is forced out when penguins swim, but they also have a layer of fat beneath the skin to keep out the cold.

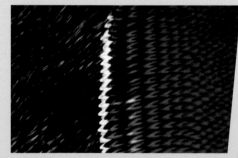

▲ Densely packed feathers of a king penguin.

A penguin's pale belly helps it escape its enemies by making it harder to see from below.

INCUBATION

King penguins breed in big colonies on rocky islands in the Southern Ocean around Antarctica. Each female lays just one large egg, which has to be incubated for seven to eight weeks. The male and female take turns, keeping the egg warm for 12 to 21 days, while the other hunts at sea. When it hatches, they also take turns keeping the chick warm for three to four months, gathering food when they are not on duty. It may be more than a year before the chick can hunt for itself.

▶ A penguin balances its egg on its large feet.

Layers of dense feathers give the penguin a streamlined body shape, saving it energy when swimming.

On average, a king penguin dives 865 times on each fishing trip.

Thick layer of insulating blubber beneath the skin

DEEP DIVER

The king penguin is the second-largest penguin species. It feeds mainly on fish, diving to 1,000 ft (300 m) or more to find them. Like all penguins, it drives itself through the water by flapping its powerful wings.

Warming waters due to climate change could make hunting much harder for king penguins, and up to 70 percent of them could vanish by 2100.

KING PENGUIN

!

The short, stiff tail is used as a prop when standing on land.

The large, webbed feet act as rudders for steering when swimming.

PENGUIN PARADE

Insulated by their thick layers of body fat and dense feathers, penguins are perfectly adapted for hunting in icy Antarctic seas and in the cold ocean currents that flow north from Antarctica toward the equator.

EMPEROR PENGUIN

The largest of the penguins at up to 4 ft (1.2 m) tall, the emperor is the only penguin that breeds on the sea ice around Antarctica. The males incubate the eggs over winter, keeping them off the ice by resting them on their feet.

ADÉLIE PENGUIN

Together with the emperor penguin, this bird breeds farther south than any other bird. Amazingly athletic, it can jump 10 ft (3 m) out of the water to land on an ice floe.

HUMBOLDT PENGUIN

This penguin hunts in the cold but food-rich Humboldt current that flows up the Pacific coast of South America and nests on nearby sandy beaches.

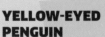

YELLOW-EYED PENGUIN

One of the world's rarest penguins, this lives on the southern coasts and islands of New Zealand. Instead of breeding in dense colonies like most penguins, it nests among scrub in isolated pairs.

ROYAL PENGUIN

Similar to the macaroni penguin, the royal penguin nests only on Macquarie Island in the Southern Ocean near New Zealand. At the end of the breeding season, the penguins leave the island to live at sea.

GALÁPAGOS PENGUIN

Although it lives on the Galápagos Islands, making it the only tropical penguin, it hunts in the cold waters of the Humboldt current that swirl around the islands.

GENTOO PENGUIN

The gentoo lives in Antarctic seas, where it feeds mainly on shrimplike animals called krill. It can swim faster than any other penguin.

MACARONI PENGUIN

One of the crested species, with flamboyant yellow head plumes, this is the most common penguin, with up to 6.3 million nesting on islands around Antarctica.

KING PENGUIN

Although it looks a lot like the emperor penguin, the king penguin is smaller at 37 in (95 cm) tall. It breeds on subantarctic islands in vast colonies that may number more than 100,000 pairs.

CHINSTRAP PENGUIN

Named for the black line that looks like the chinstrap of a hat, this penguin breeds on islands in the South Atlantic. Some pairs keep their eggs warm by nesting on the slopes of active volcanoes.

AFRICAN PENGUIN

This penguin attracts a mate with a loud call like a braying donkey, which is why it is also known by the name "jackass penguin." Some breed on the Skeleton Coast of the Namib Desert in Africa.

LITTLE PENGUIN

Just 16 in (40 cm) tall, the little penguin nests on the southern shores of Australia and New Zealand. It hunts by day, returning to land at night.

ROCKHOPPER PENGUIN

This yellow-crested penguin uses its agility to leap from rock to rock on the rugged shores that it favors for breeding. It often fights over nesting sites, slapping rivals with its flippers.

ERECT-CRESTED PENGUIN

Rare and endangered, the erect-crested penguin breeds only on a few islands off southern New Zealand. Like other penguins, it winters at sea, returning in spring to nest in large colonies on rocky ground.

MAGELLANIC PENGUIN

Common on the southern shores of South America, this relative of the Humboldt penguin is named after the explorer Ferdinand Magellan.

ICE PATROL

Floating sea ice might seem like a safe refuge for polar animals, but danger is never far away. Killer whales cruise beneath the ice, looking for victims to tip off the floes and into their gaping jaws. In the Arctic, polar bears sniff the air for prey, while in the Antarctic the dark waters conceal deadly leopard seals.

Up to 80% of crabeater seals bear the scars of leopard seal attacks.

Sensitive whiskers detect the movement of prey in the water.

Small penguins are the seal's favorite prey in summer, when the birds gather to breed.

The rear teeth lock together to form a kind of sieve, used to strain krill from the water.

When the leopard seal catches a penguin, it thrashes it around to kill it.

AMBUSH KILLER
In the Southern Ocean, predatory leopard seals lurk underwater, close to the edge of the floating ice—ready to ambush smaller seals or penguins as they slip or dive into the sea.

Powerful canine teeth give a good grip on struggling prey and are used to strip flesh.

An enormous mouth and wide gape helps the leopard seal seize big prey, such as crabeater seals.

As shrinking sea ice due to climate change affects prey, such as penguins and other seals, the long-term consequences for leopard seals are uncertain.

The front flippers help steer as the seal drives itself through the water with its tail.

LEOPARD SEAL !

WEIGHT
Up to 1,320 lb (600 kg)

CONSERVATION
Least concern

The dark gray back helps conceal the leopard seal in the water as it waits to grab prey.

The pale belly has dark spots, while the dark back has pale spots. These spots give the seal its name.

ROSS SEAL
This little-known Antarctic seal hunts squid and fish in deep, dark water beneath thick pack ice. It has unusually big eyes to help it see in the gloom.

RINGED SEAL
Found all around the Arctic, ringed seals breed on sea ice. Females hide their pups from polar bears by digging out snow caves over breathing holes in the ice.

BEARDED SEAL
The bearded seal is named for its long, sensitive whiskers, which it uses to feel for prey such as crabs and clams on shallow seabeds in the Arctic.

SOUTHERN ELEPHANT SEAL
The massively built males of this species have trunklike noses, which make their roars louder as they fight over females on the shores of sub-Antarctic islands.

CRABEATER SEAL
The branched teeth of the crabeater seal interlock to form a sieve. The seal uses this to strain krill from icy Antarctic seas.

SLEEK SEALS

With their streamlined, well-insulated bodies, seals are ideally equipped to hunt in icy water. But they cannot rear their pups at sea. Some return to the shore, while others breed on floating ice.

HOODED SEAL
Ice-breeding hooded seals live in Arctic seas around Greenland. They get their name from a strange, inflatable "hood" on the male's face.

Hood

HARP SEAL
Found in the north Atlantic and nearby Arctic Ocean, harp seals breed on floating sea ice, gathering in large colonies. They are famous for their white-furred pups.

WEDDELL SEAL
Many thousands of Weddell seals live on the Antarctic sea ice. They hunt in the deep water below and use their teeth to make breathing holes in the ice.

LEOPARD SEAL
This is the only seal that preys on other seals. It patrols the water around Antarctic sea ice, seizing and eating smaller seals and penguins.

SLEEPY GIANT

Adapted to life in the deep chill of Arctic seas, the Greenland shark lives life in the slow lane. It swims more slowly than any other fish of its size, and catches most of its prey by stealth in the deepwater gloom. By living at less than half the speed of other sharks, it manages to live more than twice as long.

Since it is cold-blooded, the shark's body is never much warmer than the surrounding icy water.

ARCTIC GIANT

The Greenland shark is one of the largest sharks, rivaling the massive and notorious great white shark in size. But its lifestyle is very different, thanks to the near-freezing water of its Arctic habitat. Young Greenland sharks grow up very slowly, taking at least 100 years to reach adulthood.

Like other sharks, the skin is dotted with thorny, toothlike scales.

CREEPING PREDATOR

The slow-moving Greenland shark is partly a scavenger that feeds on scraps and occasionally gorges on the carcass of a dead whale. One was even found with the remains of a drowned reindeer in its stomach. But despite its sluggish nature it also eats fish, seals, and even seabirds, creeping up on its prey and seizing them before they notice it.

The upper teeth are narrow spikes for gripping prey, while the lower teeth slice sideways like saw blades.

Greenland Sharks grow very slowly and females don't reproduce until the age of 100, so they are vulnerable to overfishing.

GREENLAND SHARK

!

The Greenland shark has an acute sense of smell, and electrical sensors in its snout can detect the active nerves of prey.

The eyes are often infested with small parasites that make the Greenland shark half-blind.

The first dorsal fin is unusually small for a shark.

This sluggish shark moves and breathes slowly, so has small gill slits.

A Greenland shark can probably live for more than 500 years.

WAVEWASHING

In Antarctic seas, families of killer whales often work together to catch seals resting on ice floes. Swimming together in close formation, they surge toward the ice and dive beneath it. This pushes up a wave that washes over the floating ice. The wave sweeps the seal off the floe and into the jaws of the waiting hunters. Young killer whales often accompany the adults to learn such techniques by example.

Whales spot their prey.

They push up a wave.

The wave sweeps over ice.

The seal tumbles into water.

Killer whales often raise their heads above the water to survey their surroundings. This is called spy-hopping.

Instead of having nostrils, the killer whale breathes through a single blowhole in the top of its head.

The killer whale finds fish by listening for the echoes of clicking calls focused by an organ in its forehead.

WHISTLING WHALES

Also known as orcas, killer whales live in small family groups that often travel with related families in larger groups called pods. Each pod has its own distinctive language of clicks, whistles, and calls.

Up to 52 strong, conical teeth give the killer whale a secure grip on struggling prey.

A typical killer whale is black and white, with a gray patch on its back. Each whale has a slightly different pattern.

WEIGHT
Up to 7 tons

CONSERVATION
Uncertain

FEARSOME KILLERS

One of the biggest and most powerful of all living predators, the killer whale lives in all the world's oceans. But it is most common in cold polar seas, where it hunts a variety of prey ranging from fish and seabirds to seals and even other whales. Some groups of killer whales specialize in one type of prey, using pack-hunting tactics to outwit and catch their victims.

Killer whales are threatened by pollution and hunting, but the long-term effects of climate change are uncertain.

KILLER WHALE

!

The hooked dorsal fin shows that this is a female. A male has a much taller, triangular fin.

Thick fat beneath the whale's skin keeps out the cold and gives it a streamlined shape.

A calf swims close to its mother. It will become independent at two years old, but may stay with her for life.

Killer whales sometimes kill and eat great white sharks.

The killer whale drives itself through the water by sweeping its powerful tail up and down.

REGION/HABITAT
Arctic Ocean

LENGTH
Up to 18 ft (5.5 m)

WEIGHT
Up to 1.7 tons

114

LEGENDARY TUSKS

The spectacular spiral tusk of the narwhal makes it unique among whales and instantly recognizable. In medieval Europe, narwhal tusks were sold as unicorn horns and were worth more than their weight in gold. The ivory tusk can grow to more than half the animal's body length and is used to show dominance or in fights between males.

The tusk of a big male narwhal can be up to 10 ft (3 m) long. It grows in a spiral.

About 1 in 10 female narwhals grow tusks. Very rarely, some males grow two.

Like all toothed whales and dolphins, the narwhal breathes through a single blowhole on top of its head.

ICE PODS

Small groups of narwhals, known as pods, spend the winter among the floating pack ice of the Arctic Ocean. They surface to breathe wherever there are gaps in the ice and may have to use their strength to break through. Sometimes, when the sea freezes over rapidly, they can become trapped under the ice, run out of air, and drown.

Up to 10 million sensory nerve endings in the tusk detect tiny changes in seawater salt levels.

A narwhal's muscles store oxygen in a substance called myoglobin, allowing a narwhal to dive to 4,920 ft (1,500 m) or more.

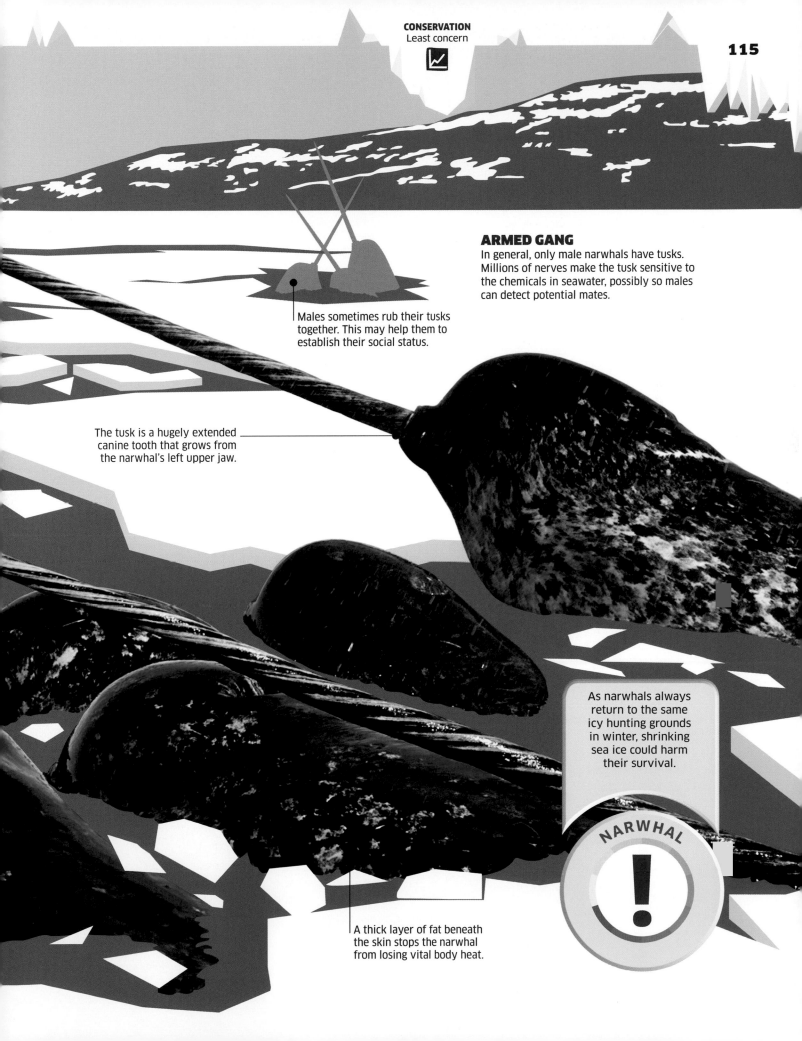

ARMED GANG

In general, only male narwhals have tusks. Millions of nerves make the tusk sensitive to the chemicals in seawater, possibly so males can detect potential mates.

Males sometimes rub their tusks together. This may help them to establish their social status.

The tusk is a hugely extended canine tooth that grows from the narwhal's left upper jaw.

As narwhals always return to the same icy hunting grounds in winter, shrinking sea ice could harm their survival.

NARWHAL
!

A thick layer of fat beneath the skin stops the narwhal from losing vital body heat.

WHITE WHALES

Unique among whales for its brilliant white skin, the beluga whale lives in the icy waters of the Arctic where it feeds on fish, squid, and shellfish such as crabs and clams. Its skin color may be an adaptation for life among the floating sea ice, helping conceal it from hungry enemies such as killer whales and polar bears.

COLD-WATER HUNTER
For much of the year, beluga whales hunt beneath and around the sea ice. They are well equipped for this, with thick body fat for insulation and acute hearing for detecting prey.

Although its eyes are adapted for seeing underwater, a beluga's vision is quite poor.

Like narwhals, the beluga sheds its worn, outer layer of skin each summer.

The forehead bulge contains an organ called a melon. It uses the echoes of the beluga's calls to locate prey and other objects.

Belugas often blow bubble rings when swimming together. These may be a form of communication.

The thick layer of fat beneath a beluga's skin accounts for half its body weight.

A beluga relies on its hearing to find prey and detect enemies.

A beluga has up to 40 small, pointed teeth, used for seizing slippery prey such as fish.

The small, rounded flippers are used for steering, as the whale drives itself along with its tail.

SINGING WHALES

Belugas are very sociable animals. They live in small groups, or pods, typically made up of about ten adults and their young, but these may come together to form huge herds of up to several thousand. They keep in constant contact using a variety of chirps, whistles, and squeaks. These white whales are so vocal that they were once called "sea canaries" after the musical songbird.

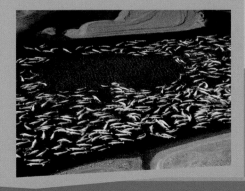

HEAVYWEIGHT JOURNEY

This humpback whale is bubble-net feeding during its annual migration—one of the longest of any mammal. Humpbacks spend spring and summer in polar waters feasting on bountiful krill and small fish. Keeping their giant mouths open, they trap large amounts of marine food and sift out unwanted seawater through their bristly baleen plates. Humpbacks eat 5,500 lb (2,500 kg) of food a day, so by fall they have all the energy necessary for their long journey ahead.

These streamlined swimmers travel at speeds of up to 5 mph (8 kph) and cover up to 5,160 miles (8,300 km) one way, with occasional stops to rest. On arrival in tropical waters, they breed and give birth to calves during the northern winter. At this time humpbacks have only their fat reserves for survival. In spring they are ready to return to their feeding grounds near the poles, and the annual cycle begins again.

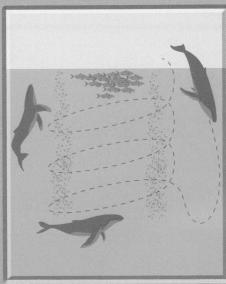

▲ Bubble-net feeding involves humpbacks blowing bubbles while swimming in a spiral formation to herd large shoals of fish into a small space.

OCEAN GIANTS

Whales are superbly adapted to life at sea, with thick layers of insulating fat that allow them to thrive in the icy polar oceans. Some are hunters, while others feed by straining small animals from the water.

BELUGA WHALE

The white-skinned beluga is one of the toothed whales—a fish hunter that lives among the ice floes of the Arctic Ocean. Like other toothed whales, it finds its prey by echolocation, like a bat.

NARWHAL

This Arctic toothed whale is renowned for its long, sharp, spirally grooved tusk, which can grow to 10 ft (3 m) long. All male narwhals have at least one tusk, and sometimes two, but only a few females have them.

GRAY WHALE

Unusually, gray whales feed on the seabed in the shallow coastal waters of the northern Pacific, sifting through mud and sand to find buried animals. They spend summer in the Arctic, then swim south for the winter.

BOWHEAD WHALE

The bowhead is a baleen whale—a type of whale with a huge mouth lined with brushlike baleen plates instead of teeth. These act as strainers, filtering small shrimplike animals from the water as the whale swims slowly through the Arctic.

HUMPBACK WHALE

Well known for its "song" and dramatic leaps from the water, this is a filter-feeding baleen whale, like the bowhead. It preys mainly on fish in both Arctic and Antarctic waters, but it migrates to warm tropical waters to breed.

KILLER WHALE

Also known as the orca, the fearsome killer whale is the most powerful oceanic hunter. It prowls both Arctic and Antarctic seas in search of prey, which ranges from large fish to seals, penguins, and even other whales.

MINKE WHALE

There are two species of this relatively small baleen whale; one is found in both Arctic and Antarctic seas, while the other is restricted to southern waters. It eats krill and small fish, and is often preyed upon in turn by killer whales.

BLUE WHALE

This gigantic baleen whale is the largest animal that has ever lived. Yet it feeds on krill, which are no bigger than a person's thumb, filtering millions of them from cool polar waters every day.

FOURHORN POACHER

This spiny scorpion fish lives on the coast of the north Pacific and nearby Arctic oceans. It feeds on the small animals it finds on sandy or stony seabeds.

CROCODILE ICEFISH

Among several Antarctic fish protected by antifreezes, icefish are also the only vertebrate animals that do not have red hemoglobin in their blood. They live by hunting smaller fish.

ARCTIC CHAR

This relative of salmon lives in lakes and coastal waters all around the Arctic. It spawns in freshwater habitats in the same way as salmon, the males turning brilliant red.

ANTARCTIC TOOTHFISH

At up to 6 ft (1.8 m) long, this is one of the biggest fish found in icy Antarctic waters. It is widely preyed on by seals, giant squid, and killer whales.

CAPELIN

Vast shoals of capelin swim in Arctic seas, feeding on the plankton that swarm near the edge of the sea ice. In turn, they are hunted by bigger fish, seabirds, and Inuit.

BURBOT

Found all around the Arctic region in lakes and rivers, the burbot often spends part of the year living under ice. A type of cod, it can grow to 4 ft (1.2 m) long.

ALPINE BULLHEAD

This small fish lives in stony Arctic and mountain streams. The male makes a nest for the eggs of several females, and guards them until they hatch.

COLD FISH

Icy polar waters are rich in oxygen and teeming with microscopic life. This makes them ideal habitats for fish that can tolerate the numbing cold. Some are even equipped with antifreeze chemicals to stop them freezing solid.

GELATINOUS SNAILFISH
The tadpolelike body of this Arctic fish is adapted to life in deep seawater that is chilled below the freezing point of fresh water. It grows to 12 in (30 cm) long.

ARCTIC GRAYLING
This freshwater fish lives in rivers and lakes in Arctic North America and Siberia. It is notable for the very large dorsal fin on its back and smells like the herb thyme.

ARCTIC COD
Living further north than any other fish, the Arctic cod is the main prey of many large polar animals including ringed seals and beluga whales.

ARCTIC SKATE
Adapted to life on the seabed, where it preys on bottom-living animals, this relative of sharks and rays lives in both Arctic and Antarctic oceans.

ARCTIC FLOUNDER
This flatfish has both eyes on the same side of its head so it can lie hidden on the sea floor, waiting to ambush prey. It lives in coastal seas all around the Arctic.

The frog stops breathing when it is frozen, but it can survive like this for several months.

FREEZING AND THAWING

A wood frog can freeze and thaw out several times each season without suffering any ill effects. This often happens at the beginning and end of winter when the temperature drops below freezing at night, but rises again by day. Repeated freeze-thaw cycles may even help the frog survive, because they stimulate the reaction that makes the frog's liver produce glucose—a sugar that protects the frog's body cells from freezing or collapsing.

The frog's heart stops beating and its blood freezes—but amazingly this does not kill it.

If no more than two-thirds of the water in the frog's body turns to ice, it will survive.

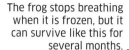

FROZEN FROGS

When winter air temperatures plunge below freezing point, many small land animals hide away in deep burrows that never freeze. But some—especially insects and a few reptiles and amphibians— are able to survive being partly frozen for weeks on end, before thawing out and carrying on with their lives. They all live in the far north—such animals do not exist in Antarctica.

LENGTH
Up to 3 in (75 mm)

WEIGHT
Up to ⅓ oz (8 g)

CONSERVATION
Least concern

125

When ice starts forming on its skin, this triggers the processes that will keep the frozen frog alive.

When the wood frog freezes, its body becomes hard and rigid, like glass.

ICE FROG

A frog cannot generate its own body heat, so if its surroundings freeze, the frog freezes, too. The American wood frog's body fluids freeze in winter, but chemicals called cryoprotectants ensure the ice crystals stay very small. The two main cryoprotectants are glucose (a kind of sugar) and a chemical called urea, which comes from the frog's urine.

SPINELESS WONDERS

Cold polar seas are rich in minerals, which allows vast numbers of tiny organisms called plankton to flourish in sunlit waters. The plankton in turn provide food for swarms of invertebrates that drift in the water or live on the seabed. Other invertebrates feed on scraps that sink to the bottom, and a few are deadly predators.

GIANT SEA SPIDER
Giant sea spiders live on the ocean floor around Antarctica and can grow up to 20 in (50 cm) wide. They prey on soft-bodied animals, stabbing them with piercing mouthparts and then sucking out the juices.

KING CRAB
Long-legged king crabs are widespread in cold oceans, where they scour the seabed for animal prey, fish eggs, and edible scraps.

GIANT SQUID
Rarely seen, this enormous animal hunts fish in the ocean depths, where it is preyed upon by sperm whales. It can grow to 43 ft (13 m) long.

ANTARCTIC SCALLOP
Like other scallops, this two-shelled mollusc feeds by filtering plankton from the water. It lives on the seabed around Antarctica, below the ice.

PROBOSCIS WORMS

Giant marine worms lurk on the Antarctic seabed. They capture prey with a long sticky tongue called a proboscis, which shoots out of the head in a split-second by turning inside out like a sock.

Jellyfish being devoured by proboscis worms.

ANTARCTIC SEA URCHIN

This spiny sea urchin is often found living alongside Antarctic scallops beneath thick sea ice. It eats other animals as well as feeding on plankton.

ANTARCTIC KRILL

Shrimplike animals called krill form vast swarms in cold oceans, especially around Antarctica, where they are the main prey of many penguins, whales, and seals.

ANTARCTIC STARFISH

This is one of the most common starfish living in icy Antarctic seas. It will eat almost anything it can find on the seabed—living or dead.

ANTARCTIC ISOPOD

Isopods look like giant wood lice. They scavenge for food on the ocean floor, eating any dead animals they can find in the cold, dark depths.

GIANT VOLCANO SPONGE

Amazingly, this animal may live for several thousand years in the icy seas around Antarctica. It feeds by filtering tiny food particles from the water.

HUMANS ON ICE

People have lived in the Arctic for thousands of years, surviving mainly by hunting and fishing. By contrast, the very existence of Antarctica was unknown to humanity before 1820, and its only long-term residents have been explorers and scientists.

For centuries, furry sealskins and other animal pelts have been used to make warm clothing.

Barbed harpoons are traditionally used to hunt seals and whales, but many Inuit now also use rifles.

Modern gear, like these ice boots, has replaced a lot of traditional Inuit equipment.

HUNTING ON ICE

The Inuit have lived in Alaska, Arctic Canada, and Greenland for a thousand years or more. For most of that time, they lived by hunting and gathering wild food. They traveled as nomads for much of the year, relying on the animals they caught to provide both food and materials for clothing, tools, and weapons.

Traditionally, most hunting was done by Inuit men, but many women were also skilled hunters.

Sea animals were hunted from small, skin-covered canoes called kayaks—a design that has been copied worldwide.

In winter, the Inuit traditionally ate nothing but meat and fish.

Temperatures are rising faster in the Arctic than almost anywhere else, melting the sea ice that is vital to the Inuit way of life.

MELTING ARCTIC !

THE WINTER HUNT

ICE FISHING
When seas and lakes freeze over in winter, the Inuit spear fish through holes cut in the ice, sometimes using lures to attract them. In open water, they fish from kayaks.

WALRUS HUNTING
Traditionally, the Inuit hunted walruses using heavy harpoons, either at sea or on the ice. The walrus was eaten, and the skins and ivory were used to make clothes, boats, weapons, and tools.

NEW LIVES
While traditional skills are still important to the Inuit, most now combine these with earning money from ordinary jobs. Many live in houses in permanent settlements, and their traditional nomadic culture is under threat.

As sea ice melts and marine animal numbers fall due to global warming, Arctic people will struggle to maintain their traditional way of life.

ARCTIC TRADITIONS

!

The Dolgan follow the reindeer on their annual migrations.

Baloks are set on skilike runners so reindeer can easily pull them across the snowy landscape. In summer, many of the Dolgan move to less mobile, wooden homes.

Tentlike homes called *baloks* are lined with warm reindeer pelts and heated by small stoves.

Dogs are good hunting companions and help herd the reindeer.

ARCTIC PEOPLE

INUIT
The indigenous people of Greenland, Canada, and Alaska are known as the Inuit. They followed the animals they hunted but now live together in small communities.

SAMI
The Sami of northern Scandinavia and Russia have lived in the Arctic for thousands of years. They once followed the reindeer but now do a variety of trades.

CHUKCHI
Small communities of Chukchi people live in Russia's easternmost region. Some still fish and hunt reindeer, although these traditions are in decline.

LIVING ON ICE

Around 4 million people call the Arctic home. Many live in modern cities and towns dotted around the coasts, but others live in more remote settlements, carrying on the traditions of their ancestors. Many Arctic people depend on hunting for survival, but as the sea ice melts earlier each year, their lifestyle is under threat.

RAISING REINDEER

The Dolgan live almost 620 miles (1,000 km) north of the Arctic Circle in Russian Siberia. They survive in some of the harshest conditions on Earth thanks to their relationship with reindeer.

To keep warm in bitter winter temperatures that can drop to –58 °F (–50 °C), the Dolgan make clothing from reindeer skins and fur.

The reindeer use their antlers and hooves to push snow and ice away so they can nibble the lichen and moss underneath.

The Dolgan herd reindeer, as well as hunting wild deer, trapping game birds, and fishing. Reindeer are their main form of transportation.

ICE HOUSE

The ingenious Inuit survived the freezing Arctic winters by using their snowy surroundings to construct igloos. As these nomadic people moved around, their homes had to be easy to build. Ice houses were crafted, in under an hour, from blocks of compacted snow with air between the crystals providing insulation. The Inuit made clothes from the pelts of reindeer and seals to keep warm. The combination of a safe shelter and cosy clothing protected against the chilling temperatures outside. Igloos are still built today, but these are usually temporary bases for hunters rather than homes.

▲ The outer wall of the igloo is marked in the snow, while a saw is used to cut multiple snow blocks.

▲ The walls are constructed by placing the snow blocks in a spiral arrangement.

▲ The blocks have a slight slope so that they stack to make a dome, with gaps for air vents.

MOUNTAINEERING

The wonder of the mountains has caught people's imagination for thousands of years. Ancient civilizations worshipped them as sacred places for their gods. By the 18th century, scientists were studying mountains, and mountaineering as a sport soon followed as climbers began scaling the summits of the world's highest peaks.

In 1975, Junko Tabei became the first woman to reach the summit of Mount Everest.

BRIDGING THE GAPS

Mountaineers sometimes have to cross gaping cracks in glacier ice, called crevasses. Large crevasses are impossible to cross without special equipment, such as collapsible ladders and ropes. However, Mount Everest has so many crevasses that aluminum ladders are laid over them permanently, ready for every mountaineer to use.

COURAGEOUS CLIMBERS

CHRIS BONINGTON
British mountaineer Sir Chris Bonington (1934–) began climbing at age 16. He successfully reached the peak of Mount Everest in 1985 and was knighted for his services to mountaineering.

REINHOLD MESSNER
Italian Reinhold Messner (1944–) was the first mountaineer to climb every mountain over 26,000 ft (8,000 m) tall. He was the first to conquer Mount Everest alone without oxygen.

LIONEL TERRAY
French climber and ski instructor Lionel Terray (1921–1965) was well known for his record-breaking climbs in the Alps. He also scaled summits in the Himalayas and Andes.

Rising temperatures are melting glaciers in many of the world's mountains, forcing climbers to find new routes to the summit.

MELTING MOUNTAINS

!

Ice axes are held in each hand to claw a route up the mountain.

Ropes are attached to ice or rock with bolts.

Climbing harness

Mountainous regions experience sudden changes in weather, with heavy snow, high winds, or dense fog often putting climbers in danger.

Several layers of windproof and waterproof clothing provide warmth in subzero temperatures.

Climbing boots have metal spikes, called crampons, to grip the ice.

MOUNTAINEERING

Mountaineering became popular in the 18th century when British climbers started tackling peaks in the Alps. The highest, Mont Blanc, was first conquered by French doctor Michel-Gabriel Paccard in 1786. All the major alpine summits had been reached by the 1870s.

THE NORTHWEST PASSAGE

Discovering a route through Arctic sea ice from the Atlantic Ocean to the Pacific Ocean proved a huge challenge for centuries. The so-called Northwest Passage was attempted by many explorers, but the maze of ice floes and treacherous weather repeatedly led to disaster. It was not until 1906 that the route was finally navigated.

Roald Amundsen learned survival skills from the Inuit – he wore reindeer skins and traveled by dog sled.

Climate change is reducing the amount of ice in the Northwest Passage, making journeys easier.

MELTING ICE

Igloos were built by Amundsen as a safe haven from the inhospitable weather.

Gjøa sailed through the many islands and ice floes of Canada's Arctic archipelago before finally reaching the Bering Strait.

The hull was reinforced to withstand collisions with sea ice.

GJØA'S GOAL

Despite being an old fishing boat, *Gjøa* was the first vessel to navigate the Northwest Passage. On board was Norwegian explorer Roald Amundsen and his crew of six. They set sail in 1903, anchored at King William Island in Canada's far north for two years, and completed the journey in 1906.

Norwegian flag

The sails were made of strong canvas to combat the fierce winds.

Small lifeboat for emergencies

The converted herring boat carried enough provisions on board to last the crew for three years.

FAILED EXPEDITIONS

MARTIN FROBISHER

English sailor Martin Frobisher tried to find the Northwest Passage in the 1570s. He got as far as Baffin Island and eventually returned to England with three Inuit captives and some iron pyrite rocks, better known as fool's gold.

HENRY HUDSON

The doomed expedition of 1610 by English navigator Henry Hudson ended when his ship became stuck in ice in the Canadian Arctic. The crew staged a mutiny during which Hudson was pushed out to sea in a tiny boat, never to be seen again.

LADY JANE FRANKLIN

In 1845, Sir John Franklin and a crew of 128 set sail to find the passage, but they never returned. Lady Jane Franklin insisted the British Navy search for her husband, leading to more than 40 expeditions, which helped to map the Canadian Arctic.

THE NORTH POLE

In the 19th century, European and American explorers turned their attention to the North Pole–the northernmost point of our planet, in the center of the Arctic Ocean. The race was on to be the first team to withstand the freezing temperatures, shifting ice, and deadly blizzards to reach the goal.

At the forefront of polar exploration was Norwegian adventurer Fridtjof Nansen and his team (above) who adopted the lifestyle of local Inuit people in their attempt on the Pole in 1893. He hunted Arctic animals for their furs and meat, as well as using powerful dogs to pull the supplies on sleds. Nansen also designed a special ship that could freeze into the ice instead of being destroyed by the floes, and his plan was to drift all the way to the pole. This vessel, named *Fram*, carried the crew on strong Arctic currents for three years, but ultimately missed the polar target.

▲ Arctic explorers Robert Peary and Matthew Henson (above) claimed to be the first people to reach the North Pole in 1909, but the claim was later disputed. The first confirmed conquest of the Pole did not take place until 1968.

RACE TO THE SOUTH POLE

The coldest continent on Earth—Antarctica—was discovered in the 18th century. At its frozen center is the South Pole, which became a target for explorers during the 20th century. Roald Amundsen finally planted the flag for Norway at the pole on December 14, 1911.

A thick, fur-lined hood helped keep out the howling, icy wind.

Wearing animal pelts was one of the many survival techniques that Amundsen adopted from the Inuit people.

Although Antarctica is warming, its main ice sheets remain intact. If all the ice were to melt, global sea levels would rise by 190 ft (58 m).

RISING SEA LEVELS

!

Polar explorers used snowshoes to spread their weight, preventing their feet from sinking into the snow.

A DEADLY CONTEST

The race for the pole began on October 19, 1911, when Amundsen's team of five men set off from their base camp with 52 dogs and 4 sleighs. They would gradually kill and eat many of the dogs, reducing the need to haul heavy supplies. British explorer Robert Falcon Scott set off 12 days later and reached the pole on January 17, 1912, only to find that Amundsen had beaten them. They faced a grueling 800-mile (1,300-km) return trek but became trapped by storms on the way back and died.

With more conventional clothes, and a scarf and balaclava to keep out the cold, Scott was less well-equipped than Amundsen.

ANTARCTIC EXPLORERS

SIR ERNEST SHACKLETON

Although British explorer Ernest Shackleton led two attempts on the South Pole, he never reached his target. His most successful trip in 1908 came within 97 miles (155 km) of the pole.

SIR JAMES CLARK ROSS

British naval officer James Clark Ross mapped a large part of the Antarctic coast between 1838 and 1843. The Ross Ice Shelf (above), Ross Island, and The Ross Sea were all named in his honor.

Roald Amundsen reached the South Pole 33 days before Robert Falcon Scott.

THE HEROIC AGE

The turn of the 20th century heralded the heroic age of Antarctic exploration. This golden era from 1898 to 1922 saw the world's bravest adventurers compete in daring expeditions to reach the poles. Careful planning, suitable clothing and equipment, and an element of luck were all needed to survive in the most challenging places on Earth.

Rising temperatures are melting Antarctic sea ice and opening routes for tourist ships. The environment is damaged when ships accidentally spill oil.

OIL SPILL

!

EXPEDITION ESSENTIALS

BOOTS
Polar explorers wore reindeer-skin boots. Lined with felt and sometimes dried grass, they provided insulation in the subzero temperatures.

SLEIGHS
Supplies were pulled on sleighs made from wood and rope. Expedition teams pulled the sleighs either by hand or using ponies and dogs for speedier travel on the ice.

SLEEPING BAGS
Reindeer pelts and sealskin were used to make insulated sleeping bags. However, when wet or frozen, these became a heavy weight to carry.

PONY SHOES
British explorer Robert Falcon Scott protected his Siberian ponies with special bamboo snowshoes, which were attached to the hooves with leather straps.

WOODEN SKIS
Long wooden skis were worn to traverse dangerous ice. A layer of wax was applied to the base of the skis for smoother and quicker movement.

FOOD RATIONS
Food was rationed to cut weight on the sleigh. The typical ration per person for a single day was a savory meat cake, crackers, butter, cocoa, sugar, and tea.

A thick hood covered most of the head to block out the cold and wind.

Clothes were loose-fitting to trap pockets of warm air and so that sweat could escape.

Oversized reindeer-fur gloves protected the hands.

A windproof outer layer covered warm clothes underneath. Layers could be easily removed to prevent overheating.

Dog sledding over the ice saved explorers time and effort.

WRAPPING UP

Polar exploration was a dangerous venture. British explorer Robert Falcon Scott spent years preparing for his 1910 expedition to the South Pole and took motorized sleighs, ponies, and dogs. Even so, the trip ended in tragedy, and Scott and his team all died on the return march.

SINKING SHIP

Antarctica was the target for intrepid explorers at the start of the 20th century. The coldest continent on Earth was the only one left to fully explore. Norwegian explorer Roald Amundsen had used skis and dogs to reach the South Pole for the first time in 1911, so Irish adventurer Sir Ernest Shackleton set himself a different goal: to cross the continent via the South Pole.

With a crew of 28, Shackleton set sail from England in August 1914. When their ship *Endurance* became stuck in the dense ice of the Weddell Sea, the crew was forced to wait for the ice to break up. Instead, the ship was crushed by ice and eventually sank ten months later. The crew escaped, crossed the treacherous ice on foot and used lifeboats from *Endurance* to reach Elephant Island. Shackleton and five crew members sailed through stormy seas for 16 days to the nearest inhabited place—a whaling station on the island of South Georgia. The crew was finally rescued from Elephant Island in August 1916.

▲ The crew's water supply came from fresh ice carried to the ship by sleigh.

ICEBREAKERS

Frozen polar seas are a major problem for tourist and transport ships. The solution is to use specially strengthened ships called icebreakers, designed to smash through the ice and create clear pathways for other vessels to use. Their huge weight, enormous size, and powerful engines combine to overcome the ice floes of the Arctic Ocean.

Icebreakers have the power to push through ice floes up to 10 ft (3 m) thick.

The high bridge (control room) provides a clear view of the route.

The icebreaker moves continuously so it doesn't get stuck in the ice.

Cranes at the front and back of the vessel are used to lift equipment and goods on board.

MARITIME TRADE

The northern sea route is an important shipping lane through icy Arctic waters. This shortcut between Europe and Asia greatly reduces the traveling distance for commercial ships, making it a cheaper and more environmentally friendly option than other routes. Global warming is likely to make this shipping lane much busier in the future.

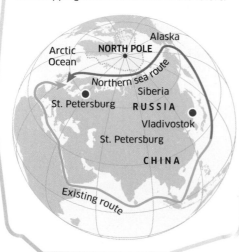

Alaska
NORTH POLE
Arctic Ocean
Northern sea route
Siberia
St. Petersburg
RUSSIA
Vladivostok
St. Petersburg
CHINA
Existing route

The pointed bow travels forward above the ice, which is crushed by the weight of the icebreaker.

The reinforced double hull is made of two watertight layers of steel.

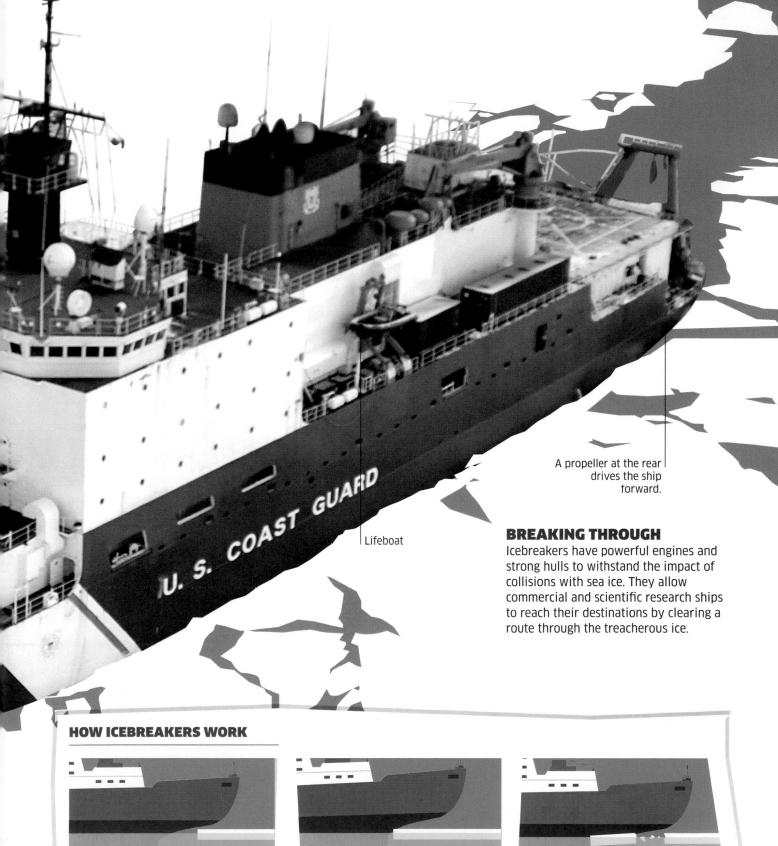

A propeller at the rear drives the ship forward.

Lifeboat

BREAKING THROUGH

Icebreakers have powerful engines and strong hulls to withstand the impact of collisions with sea ice. They allow commercial and scientific research ships to reach their destinations by clearing a route through the treacherous ice.

HOW ICEBREAKERS WORK

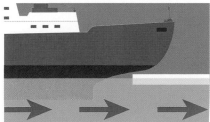

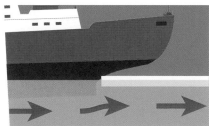

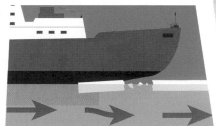

1 The pointed bow (front) of the icebreaker is the first point of contact with an ice floe.

2 The vessel glides easily over the floe and uses its great weight and power to bear down on the ice.

3 The ice breaks under the weight of the vessel, creating an ice-free path behind it for other ships to use.

POLAR RESEARCH

The Arctic and Antarctica are home to more than 150 research stations, where scientists from all over the world study the climate, wildlife, geology, and night skies of the poles. Many of the research stations are permanent buildings on land, but others are temporary structures on sea ice, and more scientists work from ships, studying sea life and the way the polar oceans interact with the atmosphere. Polar scientists have discovered that Earth's climate is changing faster at the poles than anywhere else on the planet.

DRILLING DOWN

Ice cores are collected inside hollow steel drills with a spiral blade on the outside of the drill bit. The first ice cores were taken by hand-operated drills, but today large machines are used to drill much deeper. The longest ever ice core, obtained by Russian scientists in Antarctica in 2012, was 2.3 miles (3.8 km) deep and reached ice that was more than 400,000 years old.

Steel cable

A motor inside the drill turns the blade at the bottom.

ICE CORES

The ice sheets in the Arctic and Antarctica built up over thousands of years. Scientists can study what Earth's atmosphere and climate were like in the distant past by drilling out deep cores (cylinders) of ice and analyzing the tiny air bubbles trapped inside them.

A motorized drum called a winch lifts the ice core by winding up the cable supporting it.

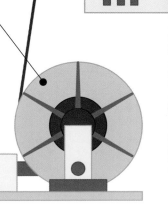

A spiral-shaped blade cuts the ice and drills downward as it rotates.

ANTARCTIC TRAVEL

There are no paved roads in Antarctica, so visitors usually travel by air, sea, or vehicles designed to move on snow and ice, such as skidoos and tractors. The Caterpillar D6N is a tractor modified to operate during the Antarctic winter in temperatures as low as −60 °F (−51 °C). Its caterpillar tracks spread the vehicle's weight better than wheels, allowing it to move over soft snow without losing grip.

The work of Antarctic scientists in the 1980s led to a worldwide ban in the use of chemicals that once caused a hole in the protective ozone layer in Earth's atmosphere.

OZONE LAYER
!

Hatch in roof for emergency escape in case the vehicle falls into a crevasse.

The wide roof provides support for a tent to keep the cabin warm.

Caterpillar tracks grip soft snow and can be fitted with metal spikes for icy surfaces.

A horseshoe-shaped boom at the front helps the tractor cross crevasses (deep cracks in the ice).

FLOATING FACILITY

HALLEY RESEARCH STATION

Antarctica's Halley research station sits on a floating ice shelf in the Weddell Sea. It consists of eight modules supported by hydraulic legs that can lift the modules when snow builds up. Skis under the legs allow the whole station to be towed to a new location if the ice under it becomes unstable.

The red module contains the communal areas for eating and relaxing.

Blue modules contain bedrooms, labs, offices, and storerooms.

CLIMATE CHANGE

The world is warming up—and in the mountains and polar regions, ice is melting. The main reason for this is the release of carbon dioxide (CO_2) when coal, oil, and other fossil fuels are burned to generate energy. The CO_2 acts like a blanket around the planet, stopping heat from escaping into space. As the oceans warm and ice melts, sea levels rise, threatening coastal cities. And as the world gets warmer, extreme weather events such as hurricanes, droughts, and wildfires are likely to become more common.

CHANGING WORLD

NATURAL DISASTERS
Rising sea levels could cause coastal erosion, leading to landslides like the one shown here. Hotter summers are also causing stormier weather and more frequent hurricanes.

ARCTIC SEA ICE 1979

One measure of climate change is the way Arctic sea ice is disappearing. This image made from satellite data shows the sea ice in the summer of 1979. It stretched right across the Arctic Ocean from Greenland to Russia.

The five warmest years since records began in 1880 have all occurred since 2003.

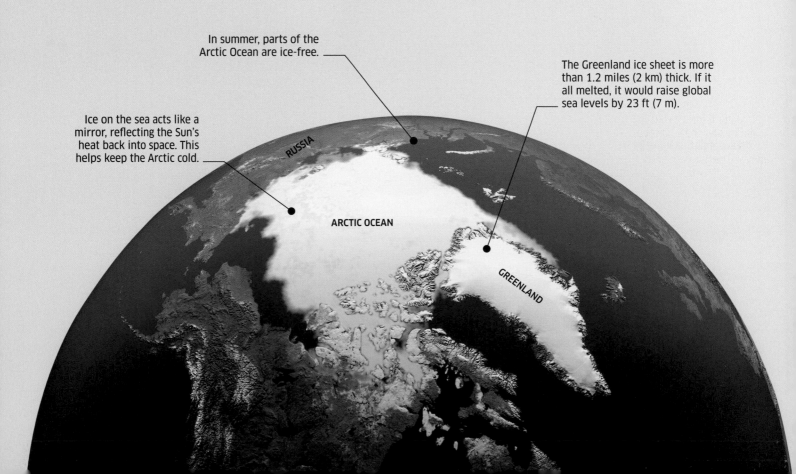

In summer, parts of the Arctic Ocean are ice-free.

The Greenland ice sheet is more than 1.2 miles (2 km) thick. If it all melted, it would raise global sea levels by 23 ft (7 m).

Ice on the sea acts like a mirror, reflecting the Sun's heat back into space. This helps keep the Arctic cold.

RUSSIA

ARCTIC OCEAN

GREENLAND

WILDLIFE

Animals adapted to particular climates may be forced to move to new areas. But those that live in the coldest places, such as polar bears, have nowhere to go and may die out.

HUMAN IMPACT

Many nations are threatened by flooding, drought, or extreme weather. If farmers lose their crops, people may starve, and the rule of law may collapse, leading to mass migration.

WHAT CAN WE DO?

We must use less energy generated by coal, oil, or gas to slow the rate of climate change. This means turning down the heating, reducing travel, and conserving energy.

ARCTIC SEA ICE 2012

Since 1979, the area covered by Arctic sea ice has been shrinking. This image shows its extent in the summer of 2012, with a huge tract of open water off Russia. Some scientists think the ice could vanish completely by 2030.

The Arctic and a part of Antarctica are warming at twice the average global rate, making the edges of ice sheets collapse and releasing icebergs into the sea.

Ground that once stayed frozen year round is now melting, releasing methane gas that accelerates global warming.

The edges of the Greenland ice sheet are melting faster in summer than ever before.

POLAR CRISIS

Melting sea ice reveals dark water that soaks up the heat of the Sun and gets warmer, keeping more ice from forming.

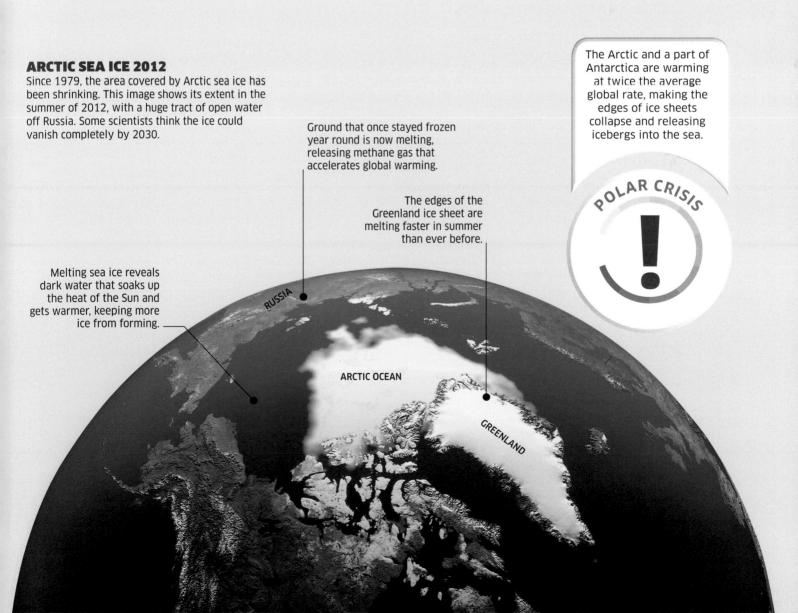

RUSSIA

ARCTIC OCEAN

GREENLAND

GLOSSARY

adaptation
The process by which a species evolves to become better suited to its surroundings.

ambush
A surprise attack by a predator on unsuspecting prey.

ancestors
Ancient animal or plant species from which recent generations have evolved.

aurora australis
A natural phenomenon in the southern hemisphere consisting of bands of colored lights in the night sky over the Antarctic region.

aurora borealis
A natural phenomenon in the northern hemisphere consisting of bands of colored lights in the night sky over the Arctic region.

avalanche
A sudden and potentially dangerous deluge of snow or ice down a mountain slope.

baleen
A fringelike structure in the mouths of some whales used to sieve food from ocean water.

blowhole
A nostril on the top of the head of a whale or dolphin.

blubber
A thick layer of fat under the skin of an animal that protects it against the cold.

breeding
The process by which animals produce offspring.

camouflage
The natural coloring or pattern of an animal's fur or skin that helps it hide by blending into the environment.

canine
The enlarged, pointed tooth of a carnivore, such as a dog or cat.

carnivore
An animal with a meat-based diet.

carrion
The fleshy remains of dead creatures.

climate change
A change in the typical pattern of weather a place experiences.

colony
A group of animals or plants living close together.

crampon
A spiked metal plate attached to a boot for walking on ice or climbing on rocks.

crevasse
A large, deep crack in a mountain or glacier.

environment
The natural surroundings in which an animal or plant lives.

expedition
A planned journey by a group of people, usually for research or exploration.

feline
Catlike, or a member of the cat family.

floe
A large area of floating ice in the sea.

fossil
The remains or traces of a plant or animal preserved in rock over thousands or millions of years.

freezing
The process by which water turns into ice at 32°F (0°C).

frost
Ice formed when water vapor in the air freezes onto solid objects.

fungus
A type of spore-producing organism that feeds on decaying organic matter or lives as a parasite on living organisms.

gene
A unit of inheritance, carried in each of an organism's cells, that came from a parent and affects or controls some aspect of how the organism looks, develops, or functions.

genetic
Caused or controlled by a gene or genes.

glacier
An accumulation of ice formed from compacted snow that moves downhill gradually.

global warming
A gradual rise in the average temperature of planet Earth.

glucose
A simple sugar that provides a source of energy for living things.

grazer
An animal that feeds on small plants such as grass.

habitat
The natural environment in which a particular animal or plant species lives.

herbivore
An animal that eats plants.

hibernation
A prolonged period of deep sleep that allows animals to remain inactive during winter.

ice
Water frozen into a solid state.

iceberg
A large mass of floating ice broken off a glacier or ice sheet.

icebreaker
A special ship that can break through sea ice. Icebreakers are used to create ice-free routes for other vessels to use.

ice shelf
A glacier that extends over the sea as a large, floating, flat-topped platform.

igloo
A permanent or temporary shelter made from snow and traditionally built by Inuits.

incisor
A cutting tooth at the front of the mouth.

incubate
The process by which a bird covers its eggs to keep them warm before the chicks hatch.

inhospitable
A challenging or hostile environment that makes it hard for animal and plant species to survive.

insulation
The process of trapping heat so it cannot escape.

Inuit
A group of indigenous people native to Greenland, Canada, and Alaska.

invertebrate
An animal without a backbone.

keratin
A protein that strengthens hair, nails, and hooves.

krill
Small, shrimplike animals found in vast quantities in the oceans and often eaten by whales.

lichen
An organism made up of a fungus and alga living closely together.

mammal
A warm-blooded animal with hair or fur that feeds its offspring with milk.

migration
The seasonal movement of animals from one area to another to find food or warmer weather.

molar
A grinding tooth at the back of the mouth.

molt
The shedding of hair or skin during the life cycle of an animal.

moss
A small green plant without flowering shoots or deep roots.

mummification
The prolonged preservation of a body.

nomadic
Animals or people who continually roam from one place to another.

organism
A living thing, such as an animal, plant, fungus, or bacterium.

permafrost
A layer of soil that stays frozen all year round.

photosynthesis
The process by which plants make food by using energy from sunlight to combine water with carbon dioxide from the air.

pigment
A natural coloring in animals or a substance used to produce color for art.

plankton
Tiny organisms that are suspended in water.

polar
Situated or living close to either the North or South Pole.

predator
A creature that hunts other animals.

prehistoric
An ancient period, before written records began.

prey
A creature that is killed by a predator for food.

proboscis
The extended nose of a creature.

sastrugi
Distinctive ridges that appear on snowy surfaces, caused by winds blowing in polar areas.

scavenger
A creature that feeds on the remains of dead animals.

species
A group of organisms that can interbreed to produce offspring.

stealth
Quiet and secretive movement intended to help an animal hunt or hide.

streamlined
Smoothly shaped to reduce resistance and aid movement through air or water.

taiga
A large belt of snowy conifer forest that runs across Earth's northern continents.

tundra
A vast, treeless habitat in polar regions that freezes in winter and thaws in summer.

translucent
Almost, but not entirely, transparent.

webbed
A foot with toes joined together by flaps of skin.

wilderness
An uninhabited and unspoiled area of our planet.

INDEX

Page numbers in **bold** refer to main entries.

ACKNOWLEDGMENTS

Dorling Kindersley would like to thank the following people for their assistance with their book: Edward Aves and Francesco Piscitelli for editorial assistance; Jagtar Singh, Vijay Kandwal, Syed Mohammad Farhan and Ira Sharma for design assistance; Simon Mumford for cartography; Alexandra Beeden for proofreading; and Helen Peters for indexing.

Picture Credits

The publisher would like to thank the following for their kind permission to reproduce their photographs:

(Key: a-above; b-below/bottom; c-center; f-far; l-left; r-right; t-top)

1 Gordon Buchanan. 2-3 Gordon Buchanan. 5 Alamy Stock Photo: Ray Wilson (crb). 8-9 Jason Roberts. 10-11 Alamy Stock Photo: All Canada Photos (tc). Florian Ledoux. 10 Alamy Stock Photo: DPK-Photo (bc). Florian Ledoux. 11 Alamy Stock Photo: Ashley Cooper pics (ca); Andrew Unangst (br). Daisy Gilardini (bc). Florian Ledoux. 12-13 Gordon Buchanan. Depositphotos Inc: ivn3da (background). 14-15 Kirsty Pargeter Vecteezy.com: (ice texture). Science Photo Library: Mikkel Juul Jensen. 15 Alamy Stock Photo: Stocktrek Images, Inc. (ca). Dorling Kindersley: Simon Mumford (bl). Science Photo Library: Mikkel Juul Jensen (crb). 16-17 Getty Images: Jean-Pierre Bouchard. 17 Alamy Stock Photo: SPUTNIK (tc). 18 Getty Images: DEA / G. DAGLI ORTI (clb). 18-19 Alamy Stock Photo: Heritage Image Partnership Ltd. 20-21 Dreamstime.com: Junichi Shimazaki. 21 Alamy Stock Photo: ITAR-TASS News Agency (tl). Dorling Kindersley: Gary Ombler / The Walled Garden, Summers Place Auction House (crb). 22 Alamy Stock Photo: Alexander Shuldiner (tl). 22-23 Roman Uchytel. 24-25 Roman Uchytel. 25 Alamy Stock Photo: Q-Images (bc). 26-27 Roman Uchytel. 28 Alamy Stock Photo: Hemis (bl). 28-29 James Kuether. 30 Alamy Stock Photo: Panther Media GmbH (clb). 30-31 Alamy Stock Photo: dotted zebra. 31 Alamy Stock Photo: John Cancalosi (tc). naturepl.com: Ole Jorgen Liodden (cra). 32-33 Gordon Buchanan. Depositphotos Inc: ivn3da (background). 34 Alamy Stock Photo: ton koene (crb). Daisy Gilardini (cl). 35 Alamy Stock Photo: imageBROKER (cb); Stocktrek Images, Inc. (cla). naturepl.com: Eric Baccega (bc). 37 Getty Images: Ashley Cooper (bl); Kevin Schafer (bc); Education Images (br). 38-39 Getty Images: Paul Harris. 40 Alamy Stock Photo: imageBROKER (cla). Thomas Kitchin & Victoria Hurst: (clb). naturepl.com: Guy Edwardes (cra). 40-41 Alamy Stock Photo: Andrew Wilson (tc). 41 Alamy Stock Photo: All Canada Photos (tc); Hilda DeSanctis (c); David Whitaker (cb); Bob Gibbons (bl). Getty Images: (cla). naturepl.com: Laurie Campbell (br). 42 Alamy Stock Photo: Minden Pictures (bl); Andrew Wilson (tr); National Geographic Image Collection (c). 42-43 Alamy Stock Photo: Laszlo Podor (bc). 43 Alamy Stock Photo: AidanStock (cra); blickwinkel (br). naturepl.com: Colin Monteath (cl). 44-45 Alamy Stock Photo: mauritius images GmbH (c); Geoff Smith (ca). 44 Alamy Stock Photo: Bill Coster (cb); Universal Images Group North America LLC / DeAgostini (cl); Irina Vareshina (br). iStockphoto.com: gubernat (clb). 45 Alamy Stock Photo: Ray Bulson (cl); louise murray (crb). iStockphoto.com: Iri_sha (bl). Dr Roger S. Key: (bl). 46 Alamy Stock Photo: Dennis Jacobsen (ca, cra). Dreamstime.com: Steve Byland (cla); Alexey Pevnev (cla); Aleksey Suvorov (br); Chris Gomersall (cb). 47 Alamy Stock Photo: blickwinkel (bl); FLPA (br). Dreamstime.com: Caglar Gungor (tl); Maria Itina (cla); Philippe Clement (c). 48-49 naturepl.com: Juan Carlos Munaz. 49 Getty Images: Stefan Christmann (crb). 50 Alamy Stock Photo: CTK (cb). naturepl.com: Nick Garbutt (cra); Dong Lei (cl); Gavin Maxwell. 51 Alamy Stock Photo: Universal Images Group North America LLC / DeAgostini (tr). naturepl.com: Francois Savigny (br); Konrad Wothe (cla); Konrad Wothe (cl). 52 Alamy Stock Photo: Dominique Braud / Dembinsky Photo Associates (bc); Cindy Carlsson (cb). Getty Images: (ca). Wikipedia: Remi Jouan (cr). 53 Alamy Stock Photo: Roy Childs (bl); Henri Koskinen (cr). Getty Images: (cra). Science Photo Library: Kenneth M. Highfill (crb). Wikipedia: Richard Fabi (cla); Jared Stanley (br). Shutterstock: David Osborn (clb); Tarpan. 54-55 naturepl.com: Colin Monteath (bc). 55 Alamy Stock Photo: Roger Clark (fcl); Zoonar GmbH (c); Keren Su / China Span (cb); Mark Weidman Photography (br). naturepl.com: Tui De Roy (tc). 56-57 Wikipedia: NSF / Josh Landis. 58 Alamy Stock Photo: Sabena Jane Blackbird (cra); World Travel Collection (crb); louise murray (br). naturepl.com: Bryan and Cherry Alexander (clb); Ingo Arndt (c). 59 Alamy Stock Photo: age fotostock (ca). 60-61 BAS: Pete Bucktrout. 61 Getty Images: Stefan Christmann (crb). 62-63 Alamy Stock Photo: Steven J. Kazlowski. 63 123RF.com: Geoffrey Whiteway (tr). Alamy Stock Photo: Radharc Images (tr). Florian Ledoux: (crb). 64-65 naturepl.com: Yva Momatiuk & John Eastcott (c). 65 naturepl.com: Andy Rouse (br). 66-67 Gordon Buchanan. Depositphotos Inc: ivn3da (background). 68-69 naturepl.com: Tony Wu. 69 Getty Images: Jenny E. Ross (crb). naturepl.com: Klein & Hubert (cra). 70-71 naturepl.com: Steven Kazlowski. 71 Alamy Stock Photo: AGAMI Photo Agency (cra); GM Photo Images (cr). naturepl.com: Steven Kazlowski (crb). 72-73 Shutterstock: andy morehouse. 74-75 naturepl.com: Michio Hoshino. 74 naturepl.com: Richard Kirby (clb). 76-77 Getty Images: Doug Lindstrand / Design Pics. 77 Getty Images: Ben Cranke (cra). naturepl.com: Wild Wonders of Europe / Munier (c). 78-79 Getty Images: Jim Cumming. 80 Alamy Stock Photo: imageBROKER (bc). naturepl.com: Morten Hilmer (cl). 80-81 Alamy Stock Photo: Our Wild Life Photography. 81 Getty Images: Jim Brandenburg / Minden Pictures (br). 82 Alamy Stock Photo: All Canada Photos (bl); André Gilden (bc); Kostya Pazyuk (cr). Getty Images: Steven Kazlowski (cl). 83 Getty Images: Matthias Breiter / Minden Pictures. 84 Getty Images: Robert Postma. 85 Alamy Stock Photo: Robert McGouey / Wildlife (bl); Prisma by Dukas Presseagentur GmbH (bc); Minden Pictures (br). Getty Images: Joel Sartore (c). 86-87 Alamy Stock Photo: Abeselom Zerit. 87 Alamy Stock Photo: Avalon / Photoshot License (crb); Danita Delimont (cr). Dorling Kindersley: Wildlife Heritage Foundation, Kent, UK (bc). naturepl.com: Gavin Maxwell (cra). 88-89 Alamy Stock Photo: Juniors Bildarchiv GmbH. 89 Alamy Stock Photo: All Canada Photos (tl); Stocktrek Images, Inc. (tr). naturepl.com: Gerrit Vyn (tc). 90-91 naturepl.com: Kerstin Hinze. 91 Alamy Stock Photo: Michelle Gilders (crb); MichaelGrantBirds (cra); Zoonar GmbH (cr). 92-93 Alamy Stock Photo: Kevin Schafer. 92 Alamy Stock Photo: Derren Fox (c). Getty Images: Paul Nicklen (bl). naturepl.com: E.J. Peiker (tr). 94-95 naturepl.com: David Tipling. 95 Alamy Stock Photo: AGAMI Photo Agency (bl); Karen van der Zijden (cl); All Canada Photos (cr); Arco Images GmbH (br). 96 Alamy Stock Photo: Design Pics Inc (cla); Minden Pictures (tc); Dmytro Pylypenko (c). Depositphotos Inc: mikeland45 (tr). naturepl.com: Andy Rouse (cra). Shutterstock: Jo Crebbin (tr); Jo Crebbin (cl). 97 Alamy Stock Photo: Arterra Picture Library (cr); Minden Pictures (cra); Vasiliy Vishnevskiy (bl). Depositphotos Inc: lifeonwhite (c). Getty Images: Sjoerd Bosch (tl). naturepl.com: Paul Hobson (tr). Shutterstock: BMJ (cr); polarman (clb). 98-99 Dorling Kindersley: Dreamstime.com: Vladimir Melnik / Zanskar. 98 Alamy Stock Photo: All Canada Photos (c). 100-101 naturepl.com: Tony Wu. 101 Getty Images: Paul Nicklen (bl). 102-103 naturepl.com: Hiroya Minakuchi. 102 naturepl.com: Tui De Roy. 103 Alamy Stock Photo: Accent Alaska.com (c). 104 Dorling Kindersley: Dreamstime.com: Jan Martin Will (cra); Dreamstime.com: Andreanita (bc); Jan Martin Will (cla); Isselee (c); Nyker1 (crb). 105 Alamy Stock Photo: Galaxiid (bc). Dorling Kindersley: 123RF.com: Dmytro Pylypenko / pilipenkod (fcl). Dreamstime.com: David Dennis (cr); Sergey Korotkov (cla); Richard Lindie (ca); Isselee (cl); Jason Ondreicka (br). 106 Alamy Stock Photo: Stocktrek Images, Inc. (bl). 106-107 Alamy Stock Photo: Vladimir Seliverstov. 108 Alamy Stock Photo: AGAMI Photo Agency (cla); Philip Mugridge (cr); Science History Images (c). Shutterstock: Sergey 402 (tc); vladsilver (bc). 109 Alamy Stock Photo: imageBROKER (ca); Papilio (bl). Shutterstock: Enrique Aguirre (cra); Volodymyr Goinyk (cl). 110 Alamy Stock Photo: Doug Perrine (bc). 110-111 SeaPics.com: Saul Gonor (c); Saul Gonor (b). 111 SeaPics.com: Saul Gonor (t). 112 naturepl.com: Kathryn Jeffs (cl). 112-113 Alamy Stock Photo: Panther Media GmbH. 113 Alamy Stock Photo: Benny Marty (cr). 114 naturepl.com: Flip Nicklin (bc). 114-115 National Geographic Creative: Paul Nicklen. 116-117 Alamy Stock Photo: Paul Souders. 117 Alamy Stock Photo: Minden Pictures (bc). naturepl.com: Hiroya Minakuchi (c). 118-119 Getty Images: Eastcott Momatiuk. 120 Alamy Stock Photo: Minden Pictures (cla); KEN VOSAR (tr); robertharding (c); Nature Picture Library (bl). 120-121 Alamy Stock Photo: WaterFrame. 121 Alamy Stock Photo: robertharding (cr); Wildestanimal (cla); RooM the Agency (cra). 122 Alamy Stock Photo: blickwinkel (tc); Minden Pictures (tl); Zoonar GmbH (cl); YAY Media AS (bl); Juniors Bildarchiv GmbH (br); YAY Media AS (cra). Getty Images: Aurora Photos (c). Catherine W. Mecklenburg: (tr). 123 Alamy Stock Photo: Andrey Nekrasov (bc). Peter Leopold: (cla). Catherine W. Mecklenburg. naturepl.com: David Shale (clb). 124-125 Wikipedia: Brian Gratwicke. 124 Brett Amy Thelen: (clb). 126 Erwan AMICE: (br). NOAA: Monterey Bay Aquarium Research Institute (cr). Science Photo Library: British Antarctic Survey (cra). 127 Alamy Stock Photo: imageBROKER (tr); Minden Pictures (c); WaterFrame (cb); Minden Pictures (c); Stocktrek Images, Inc. (cra). Stacy Kim: (bl). 128-129 Gordon Buchanan. Depositphotos Inc: ivn3da (background). 130 Getty Images: Gordon Wiltsie. 131 Alamy Stock Photo: Cavan Images (crb); robertharding (tc); imageBROKER (cr). 132-133 naturepl.com: Bryan and Cherry Alexander. 132 naturepl.com: Bryan and Cherry Alexander (bl); Bryan and Cherry Alexander (bc); Bryan and Cherry Alexander (br). 134-135 Joel Heath / peopleofafeather.com. 136 Alamy Stock Photo: imageBROKER (cr); TCD / Prod.DB (cb); Keystone Press (crb). Chris Bonington: (clb). 137 Alamy Stock Photo: Image Source Plus. 138-139 Dorling Kindersley: Geoff Brightling / Scott Polar Research Institute, Cambridge. 139 Alamy Stock Photo: Archivart (b); The Picture Art Collection (br). Getty Images: Stock Montage (cr). 140-141 Alamy Stock Photo: Granger Historical Picture Archive. 142 Alamy Stock Photo: Everett Collection Inc (bl). 142 Alamy Stock Photo: Everett Collection Inc (cr). 143 Alamy Stock Photo: Chronicle (c); IanDagnall Computing (tr). naturepl.com: Michel Roggo (cr). 144 Alamy Stock Photo: 914 collection (cb); The Print Collector (cl); The Print Collector (c); Sean Smith (c); The Print Collector (clb); The Print Collector (crb). 145 akg-images. 146 Getty Images: Scott Polar Research Institute, University of Cambridge (clb). 146-147 Getty Images: Scott Polar Research Institute, University of Cambridge. 148-149 Alamy Stock Photo: US Coast Guard Photo. 150 Getty Images: Carsten Peter / National Geographic (tl). 152 Alamy Stock Photo: robertharding (cra); Science History Images (bc). 153 Alamy Stock Photo: Robert Matton AB (cra); Science History Images (bc). naturepl.com: Bryan and Cherry Alexander (ca); Eric Baccega (cla)

All other images © Dorling Kindersley
For further information see: www.dkimages.com